Editor
Jennifer Overend Prior, M.S. Ed.

Managing Editor
Ina Massler Levin, M.A.

Editor-in-Chief
Sharon Coan, M.S. Ed.

Illustrator
Ken Tunell

Cover Artist
Denice Adorno

Art Coordinator
Denice Adorno

Imaging
James Edward Grace

Product Manager
Phil Garcia

Publishers
Rachelle Cracchiolo, M.S. Ed.
Mary Dupuy Smith, M.S. Ed.

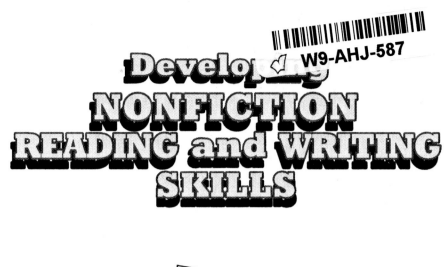

Developing NONFICTION READING and WRITING SKILLS

Authors

Betty Weiss, M.S. and Sheila Greenberg, M.S.

Teacher Created Materials, Inc.
6421 Industry Way
Westminster, CA 92683
www.teachercreated.com
ISBN-1-57690-3083-5
©2000 Teacher Created Materials, Inc.
Reprinted, 2002
Made in U.S.A.

Table of Contents

Introduction

Philosophy of Reading

Language Arts curricula across the United States is composed of various elements: reading, writing, grammar, listening, and speaking. This book is designed as a tool for teachers of grades four through six to use in developing writing skills in coordination with reading, specifically nonfiction selections, relating to other nonfiction or fictional passages.

National and state tests in the area of English Language Arts have reflected the needed emphasis on students' abilities to read, comprehend, and write in response. Students must be proactive readers. Nonfiction reading passages require students to read, question, understand, and react. The first level of reading is knowledge based. Students must be able to recall information and identify detail. In addition, comprehension of the material requires the ability to explain the information presented. Higher levels involve applying the information to self and others and analyzing the information. The transference of knowledge to other areas of academic learning brings students to yet a higher level of ability. They can then use the information gained to create new products. At the highest level of thinking, students should be able to evaluate their readings and support their opinions with specific examples, factually documented and personally substantiated.

How to Use the Book

This book has been formatted in the same manner that many new state and national standardized tests have been designed. Many of the paired reading passages are strictly nonfiction, whether content-oriented or biographical. Some of the nonfiction passages are matched with fictional reading selections, myths, and legends.

The strength of a young reader develops with growth in comprehension skills, literary and interpretive skills, and evaluative skills. Being able to coordinate and correlate diverse reading materials around a general theme displays high levels of thinking, reading, and writing skills.

In this introduction, you will find a guided model of instruction and rubrics for grading. The remainder of the book contains a wide variety of practice exercises.

Introduction *(cont.)*

The readings are divided among three different curriculum areas: social studies; interdisciplinary humanities; and science, math, and technology. Each activity consists of two related reading selections. They are followed by writing activities. Some type of visual organizer must first be completed. Then, the student is required to answer two short response questions, each relating to one of the passages. Finally, the student must complete an essay related to both passages and incorporate personal experience. The teacher may use each activity in segments, or as a whole, as testing conditions would impose upon the student.

To the Student

This book has been designed to help you better understand nonfiction readings and to develop your ability to respond by writing your explanations on various types of questions. Each activity consists of two reading selections, a graphic organizer following a question, two short response questions, and an essay.

The two readings are generally paired nonfiction selections. At times, the nonfiction selection is paired with a fiction selection that is based on a similar theme. The graphic organizer requires note-taking skills to respond to the question. The two short responses require attention to detail, understanding of literature, and drawing conclusions. The essay question generally requires a written reaction involving supporting details from both readings. Specific guidelines follow the essay and can easily be identified by the bullets with which they are marked. In all cases, you should refer back to the reading selections as often as needed.

Quality essays often require a specific format. They should include a topic sentence and a concluding sentence. Each bulleted item must be addressed along with supporting details and examples. All guidelines for good writing should be followed—correct spelling, punctuation, grammar, sentence structure, and paragraphing.

The Model

Note To the Teacher: Below you will find a model selection about Sammy Sosa and Roberto Clemente. Acceptable responses have been included after the entire activity.

Baseball Giants

Read the articles about two famous Hispanic baseball players. The first biographical sketch is about Sammy Sosa, and the second is about Roberto Clemente.

First you will complete a chart and answer two short-response questions. Then you will write an essay about both articles. You may look back at the articles as often as necessary.

Sammy Sosa

Sammy Sosa was born in San Pedro de Macoris, Dominican Republic, on November 12, 1968. Like many children in his country, Sammy loved baseball; and also like many children in his country, Sammy couldn't afford real baseball equipment. He and his friends made gloves from milk cartons, bats from tree branches, and balls from old socks and tape. Sammy worked hard for little money selling orange juice and shining shoes in order to spend his free time playing baseball. Even though he was very skinny and hadn't touched a real baseball bat until he was 14, Sammy was signed by the Texas Rangers when he was 16 years old. The Rangers paid him $3,500. He sent $3,300 of that money back to his family in the Dominican Republic.

Sammy struggled with the Rangers and was soon traded to the Chicago White Sox. He struggled with his new team as well, and it appeared that the boy who had devoted his life to baseball would have to return home without enough money to help his family out of poverty. Then, Sammy's fortune changed. In 1992 he was traded to the Chicago Cubs. There, the once-skinny Sosa worked hard to become strong, and he started hitting

The Model *(cont.)*

the ball with a lot of power. In his first full year as the Cubs' right fielder, Sammy hit 33 home runs—more than twice as many as he had hit in any previous season. Sammy continued to play well for the Cubs, and in 1997 he was rewarded with a $42-million contract. But that was just the beginning of Sammy's success on the field.

Prior to 1998, the record for home runs in a single season was 61. But that year, Sammy and Mark McGwire both broke the record. The baseball world watched as the two fought a close and exciting battle for the home run crown. Even though Sammy and Mark were competing against each other, they became good friends and rooted for each other to have success. McGwire ended up slugging 70 homers, and Sammy was a close second with 66. That year, Sammy won the National League's Most Valuable Player award as he led the Cubs into the playoffs. In 1999 Sammy and

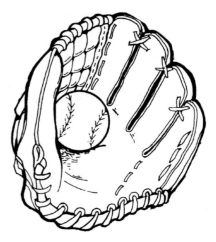

Mark were at it again. Sammy finished the season with 63 home runs, and Mark hit 65. Finally, in 2000, Sammy led the major leagues in home runs with 50. His hard work had paid off.

Sammy has been as amazing off the field as he has been on it. He has started several programs, such as the Sammy Sosa Foundation, that help the poor and hungry of the world. In December of 1997 he went on a seven-city Sammy Claus tour of the United States in which he gave presents to thousands of children in schools and hospitals. The next year, Sammy flew food and supplies to his native Dominican Republic when it was struck by a terrible hurricane. In 1998 Sammy was awarded for his good deeds when he was presented with the Roberto Clemente Man of the Year Award. It is the highest honor major league baseball gives to those who are great ballplayers and great citizens, too. Sammy Sosa definitely fits that description.

The Model *(cont.)*

Roberto Clemente

Roberto Clemente loved baseball. As a young child growing up in Carolina, Puerto Rico, he played at every opportunity. While listening to the radio, he would squeeze a ball to build up muscles in his throwing arm. When he was in his bedroom, he would bounce a rubber ball off the wall to practice catching. When he and his friends were unable to buy real baseballs, they made their own from old golf balls, string, and tape.

As Roberto grew older, he practiced more and became a better baseball player. His first job playing baseball was with the Santurce Crabbers. Roberto was offered a job with the Brooklyn Dodgers, but his father said he had to finish school.

After completing his schooling, Roberto Clemente went to Montreal, Canada, to play on a farm team. He was soon discovered there by the Pittsburgh Pirates. They asked him to play right field for their team. Roberto gladly accepted.

As a Pirate, Roberto was on two World Series championship teams. He was the Most Valuable Player of the National League in 1966. He had 3,000 hits in his career. As a champion, Roberto never forgot his fans. To show his love for them, he thanked the fans by doing good deeds. He donated money to people in need, and he spent time visiting sick children. When an earthquake struck Nicaragua, Roberto Clemente spent the Christmas holiday collecting supplies for the victims. He was flying from Puerto Rico to Nicaragua on December 31, 1972, to deliver the supplies. However, shortly after the plane took off, it crashed. Roberto and everyone else on board died.

Roberto was missed by many people. Three months after he died, he was voted into the Baseball Hall of Fame. Roberto's father wanted him to be a good man. Roberto Clemente proved to be a great man.

The Model *(cont.)*

A. Compare Sammy Sosa and Roberto Clemente by completing the Venn diagram. Include ideas about their similarities and differences. You may wish to discuss where they were born, where they were raised, for whom they played, honors they received, etc. Use details from the reading selections.

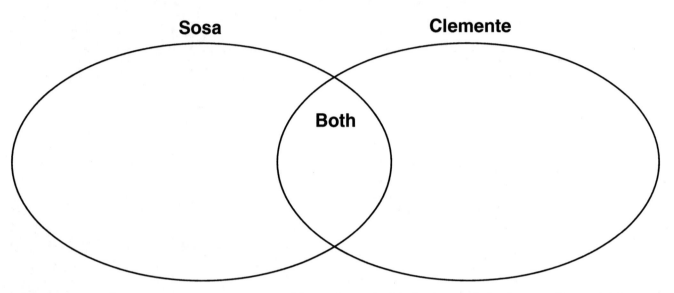

Sosa **Clemente**

Both

B. Sammy Sosa grew up very poor. How do you think that might have affected his off-the-field charity work when he became a rich man?

_____

_____

_____

C. Do you think that Roberto Clemente's father was correct when he insisted that his son complete his schooling before entering the world of baseball? Explain.

_____

_____

_____

Planning Section

Use the space below or on the back to plan your response to the essay question that appears on the following page. You may use a graphic organizer or web to help you plan your essay. Write your final essay on a separate piece of paper.

The Model *(cont.)*

Essay

Both Sammy Sosa and Roberto Clemente were very successful baseball players. Explain why you feel they were able to reach the level of success they achieved. Use information from both reading selections.

In your response, be sure to include:

- ★ two character traits for each person
- ★ one obstacle each person overcame
- ★ what quality is needed most to succeed

Check your essay for proper spelling, grammar, and punctuation.

_____

_____

_____

_____

_____

_____

_____

_____

Answer Key

A. Sammy Sosa: born in San Pedro de Macoris, Dominican Republic, in 1968; has played on three different teams; is known for his home run hitting; twice hit over 60 home runs in a season.

B. Roberto Clemente: grew up in Puerto Rico; did hand and arm strengthening exercises; played with the Santurce Crabbers; refused a job with the Brooklyn Dodgers to finish his education; played on a farm team; played for the Pirates; voted into the Baseball Hall of Fame after his death.

   Both: Couldn't afford baseball equipment when they were young; played right field; won Most Valuable Player award; did a lot of charity work; etc. (Accept all reasonable answers.)

B. (Accept all reasonable answers.) Because he grew up poor, Sammy understood the value of money and the importance of helping those less fortunate than himself. His contributions have meant a lot to the people of the Dominican Republic and the United States.

C. (Accept all reasonable answers.) Yes, because if he was not successful as a ball player, he would still be able to get a job. No, because his father may have caused him to miss a great opportunity that he would never again receive.

Essay—Accept all reasonable answers.

Rubrics for Grading

In this section, you will find several rubrics for grading. One rubric is for grading holistically on a 0–4 basis for comprehension of information. Another rubric is to be used for grading writing style, grammar, and spelling. A third rubric has been included for use in grading both by letter grade and number grade.

Numeric and Percentage Grading Rubric

90 to 100	=	A- to A+
80 to 89	=	B- to B+
70 to 79	=	C- to C+
60 to 69	=	D- to D+

The Visual Organizer (Item A)	=	10 points
Short Response Question (Item B)	=	20 points
Short Response Question (Item C)	=	20 points
The Essay Question	=	50 points

Writing Mechanics Rubric

Spelling, Punctuation, and Style

4 Reflects excellent control of language with a few errors. Paragraphing, punctuation, spelling, capitalization, syntax, and grammar are correct and any errors are minimal. Sophisticated use of vocabulary.

3 Responses reflect good control of language with some errors. Paragraphing, punctuation, spelling, capitalization, syntax, and grammar are mostly correct, although there are some errors. Good use of vocabulary.

2 Exhibits several errors in paragraphing, punctuation, spelling, capitalization, syntax, and grammar. Vocabulary is adequate.

1 Responses reflect minimal control of language with many errors that interfere with the readability and understanding. Many errors demonstrate little comprehension of the material.

0 Lack of control demonstrates no comprehension. The writing is unintelligible.

Comprehension/Writing Rubric

Short Response and Essay

4

★ Response addresses most of requirements with accuracy, comprehension, elaboration of details, and examples.
★ Response is logical and well developed.
★ The response uses insightful vocabulary.
★ Demonstrates high level of interpretation.

3

★ Response addresses some of the question and key points, but is brief, lacking elaborate detail and examples.
★ Generally focused with some mistakes.
★ Demonstrates moderate level of interpretation.

2

★ Response answers some of the question correctly.
★ Response has some relevant details, connections, and examples, but they are weak and unfocused.
★ Demonstrates some level of interpretation.

1

★ Few correct details exist.
★ The response is minimal.
★ The response is sketchy.
★ Demonstrates little interpretation.

0

★ Response is blank, disjointed, inappropriate, and incorrect.
★ Demonstrates no understanding.

National Holidays

Read the articles entitled "Mother's Day" and "Father's Day." Both articles discuss the historical background of these national holidays.

You will complete a chart and answer two short response questions about the reading selections. Then you will write an essay about the two articles. You may look back at the articles as often as you like.

Mother's Day

At the urging of Anna Jarvis of Grafton, West Virginia, Mother's Day was first celebrated on a large scale on May 10, 1908.

A day called Mothering Sunday originated in England many years ago. It took place in the middle of the Lenten (pre-Easter) season each year. Julia Ward Howe, the author of "The Battle Hymn of the Republic" and suffragette, first suggested a Mother's Day in the United States in 1872. She thought the day should be dedicated to the observance of peace. For several years, she held annual observances of the day in Boston, but it did not gain national support. In 1887, a Kentucky teacher named Mary Towles Sasseen began annual Mother's Day celebrations, and in 1904 Frank E. Hering of Indiana did the same. But it was not until three years later that the interest was ignited in Anna Jarvis, and she began a campaign for the national observance of the holiday. She selected the second Sunday in May for the celebration. In May of 1908, churches in Grafton and Philadelphia began the tradition. A Grafton church devoted its service to the memory of Jarvis's mother, Anna Reeves Jarvis.

The Methodist Episcopalian Church, to which Anna Jarvis belonged, designated her as the founder of Mother's Day at a conference in 1912, and the conference also adopted her chosen date of the second Sunday in May for the observance. In May of 1914, President Woodrow Wilson signed a resolution recommending that the government recognize and observe Mother's Day, and in 1915 it was declared a national holiday.

Anna Jarvis began one more Mother's Day tradition. On the first Mother's Day, she wore a carnation in memory of her mother. Traditionally, people wear colored carnations if their mothers are living and white if they are not. Today, families in the United States have developed their own additional traditions that include cards, flowers, candy, gifts, and sharing mealtime with the whole family.

National Holidays *(cont.)*

Father's Day

When Sonora Louise Smart Dodd of Spokane, Washington, heard a sermon at her church concerning Mother's Day, she got the idea for a day to honor fathers in the same way. Dodd wished especially to honor her own father, William Jackson Smart, who had raised his six children alone after his wife died in 1898.

The young woman began a petition recommending that Spokane adopt an annual Father's Day celebration. She also got the support of the Spokane Ministerial Association and the Young Men's Christian Association (YMCA). Dodd's efforts were finally successful, and on June 19, 1910, the first Father's Day was celebrated in Spokane.

After that time, many people and groups tried to make the day a national holiday; it was not until 1972 that President Richard Nixon signed the day into law.

Today, Father's Day is celebrated around the world. In the United States and Canada, it falls on the third Sunday in June. On that day, people honor their fathers with gifts, cards, and special tributes.

National Holidays *(cont.)*

A. Use the web to show which people are recognized as having an impact on the celebration of Mother's Day as a national holiday.

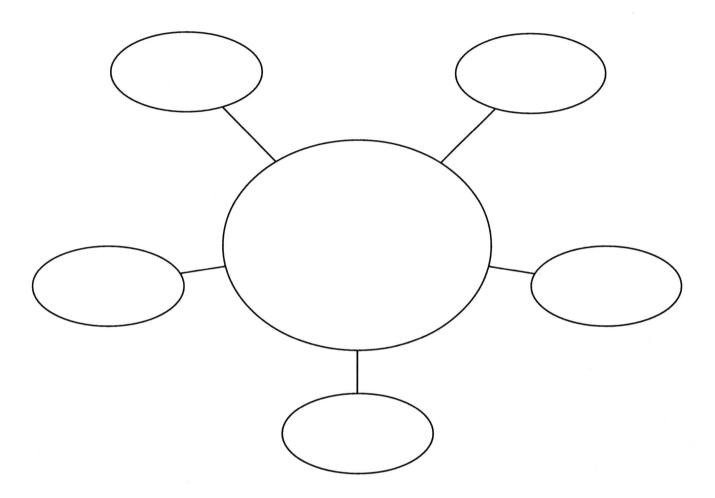

B. How did Mother's Day become a national holiday?

_____

_____

_____

_____

_____

_____

_____

_____

National Holidays *(cont.)*

C. How did Spokane, Washington come to celebrate the first Father's Day?

_____

_____

_____

_____

_____

_____

_____

Planning Section

Use the space below to plan your response to the essay question that appears on the following page. You may use a graphic organizer or web to help you plan your essay. Write your final essay on the lines provided below the essay question.

National Holidays *(cont.)*

Essay

Mother's Day and Father's Day have been declared national holidays in the United States in order to pay tribute to parents. Discuss each holiday and the characteristics that make a good mother or father. Use details from both reading selections.

In your response, be sure to include:

★ an introduction naming the holidays and when they are celebrated

★ characteristics you feel make a good mother and father, citing specific examples

★ a conclusion explaining general and/or your own traditions associated with each holiday

Check your essay for proper spelling, grammar, and punctuation.

_____

_____

_____

_____

_____

_____

_____

_____

_____

_____

_____

_____

_____

Female Civil Rights Leaders

Read the articles entitled "An Extraordinary Bus Ride" and "Underground Railroad Leader." The articles explain the roles of Rosa Parks and Harriet Tubman in the fight for African-American civil rights in the United States.

You will complete a chart and answer two short-response questions about the reading selections. Then you will write an essay about the two articles. You may look back at the articles as often as you like.

An Extraordinary Bus Ride

She has been called the mother of the Civil Rights movement, but Rosa McCauley Parks did not consider herself to be extraordinary. Born on February 4, 1915, in Tuskegee, Alabama, McCauley had a normal childhood. She grew up on a farm and attended an all-black school in her neighborhood. Her high-school education was cut short by her mother's death, but she finished her schooling after her marriage to Raymond Parks. In 1943 she joined the NAACP (National Association for the Advancement of Colored People) and worked with the Voters' League, registering African Americans to vote. Then came the fateful day.

The bus ride on December 1, 1955, began as usual. After completing her job as a seamstress for a Montgomery, Alabama, department store, Parks boarded the bus to go home. As was required, she took a seat in the back of the bus. When all the seats filled up, Parks was asked to vacate hers for a white man who was just getting on the bus. (At that time in Montgomery, the law required blacks to sit at the back of the bus and to give up their seats for white people when all other seats were filled.) On this day, however, Parks refused to move. The bus driver stopped the bus and called for policemen, who whisked her away to jail. NAACP leader Edgar Daniel Nixon posted her bail and determined that Rosa Parks would be the last African American arrested for such an action.

Female Civil Rights Leaders *(cont.)*

An Extraordinary Bus Ride *(cont.)*

Along with other black leaders, including Dr. Martin Luther King, Jr., Nixon declared a one-day boycott of all city buses. Leaflets announcing the boycott were distributed throughout the city. On the appointed day, the results were dramatic. Not one African American rode on any buses there. Because it was such a success, the boycott was extended indefinitely.

For their actions, blacks were harassed on the street, hundreds of their leaders were arrested, and many lost their jobs. Still, the boycott continued with African Americans turning to alternative modes of transportation, including walking, carpooling, riding bicycles, and even riding mules. The boycott ended when, after 381 days, the U.S. Supreme Court ruled in favor of Rosa Parks and declared Alabama bus segregation laws unconstitutional. The boycott had cost the bus company $750,000 in lost revenues, but the gains in human dignity were priceless.

Female Civil Rights Leaders *(cont.)*

Underground Railroad Leader

Harriet Tubman was born a slave in Dorchester County, Maryland. The exact date of her birth is unknown, but it is believed that she was born around 1820. When she was a young girl, she tried to block a doorway to stop her master from beating another slave. Her master threw an iron weight to get her to move. The weight hit her in the head, and she fell unconscious on the floor. For the rest of her life, Tubman suffered from daily blackouts that were a result of this injury.

Tubman learned that her master planned to send her further south, where she knew life would be even worse. Rather than endure the hardships of slavery any longer, she decided to escape to the North. She knew the journey would be a dangerous one. She had heard other slaves tell stories about the Underground Railroad, which was a network of roads, underground tunnels, and homes that were used to take slaves to freedom. The Underground Railroad was run by abolitionists, people who believed that slavery was wrong and worked to end it. Tubman used the Underground Railroad to get to Philadelphia, Pennsylvania, where she was finally free.

Tubman got a job as a maid and worked hard to save some money. She wanted to bring her brothers and sisters to freedom. In 1851, Tubman joined the abolitionists and started leading expeditions of slaves from the South to the North. She did not worry about her personal safety. The safety of the escaping slaves was all that was important to her. Over a fifteen-year period, Tubman helped 300 slaves escape.

Tubman worked for the Union Army during the Civil War. She took jobs as a cook, nurse, and even a spy. Her heroic efforts led to the rescue of 756 slaves and the destruction of enemy property. Although many rewards were offered by slave masters for the capture of Harriet Tubman, she remained free. She continued to help people in need until her death on March 10, 1913.

Female Civil Rights Leaders *(cont.)*

A. Choose four words that would describe either Rosa Parks or Harriet Tubman.

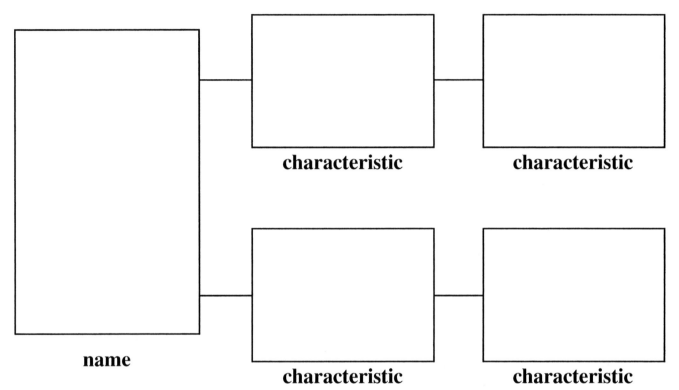

name

characteristic   characteristic

characteristic   characteristic

B. What were the four major events that occurred after Rosa Parks got on the bus on December 1, 1955 in Montgomery, Alabama? Be certain to explain the events in sequential order.

_____

_____

_____

_____

_____

_____

_____

_____

_____

Female Civil Rights Leaders *(cont.)*

C. How did Harriet Tubman escape from slavery?

_____

_____

_____

_____

_____

_____

_____

_____

_____

_____

_____

Planning Section

Use the space below to plan your response to the essay question that appears on the following page. You may use a graphic organizer or web to help you plan your essay. Write your final essay on the lines provided below the essay question.

Female Civil Rights Leaders *(cont.)*

Essay

Rosa Parks and Harriet Tubman made decisions that helped change history. What choices did they make and how was history affected by their decisions? Use information from both reading selections.

In your response, be sure to include:

★ a description of each person

★ choices each person made

★ how history changed as a result of each of their choices

Check your essay for proper spelling, grammar, and punctuation.

_____

_____

_____

_____

_____

_____

_____

_____

_____

_____

_____

_____

Power of Women

Read the article entitled "Three First Ladies" about three Presidents' wives during the 1970s. Then read the article about the Equal Rights Amendment (ERA), which was supposed to guarantee equality of opportunity for women.

You will complete a chart and answer two short-response questions about the reading selections. Then you will write an essay about the two articles. You may look back at the articles as often as you like.

Three First Ladies

During the 1970s there were three First Ladies—Pat Nixon, Betty Ford and Rosalynn Carter. Each had a distinctive personality and brought a different flare to the White House.

Pat Nixon

When Pat Nixon became first lady, she was the mother of two teenage daughters, Tricia and Julie. Continuing in the tradition of Jackie Kennedy, Mrs. Nixon proceeded with the renovation of the White House to make it a museum of American heritage. In addition, she supported the cause of volunteerism and urged Americans to get involved with their communities. Her greatest political success was as a goodwill ambassador on trips to Africa. Pat Nixon died in 1993 and is buried beside her husband in Yorba Linda, California, at the Richard Nixon Library and Birthplace.

Betty Ford

Betty Ford is most remembered for her candidness in her personal life. When she spoke publicly about her battle with breast cancer, she raised public awareness of the disease and served as an inspiration to others who faced cancer. As first lady, Betty Ford also supported the Equal Rights Amendment and valued both the traditional role of women and the role of women in the workplace. After leaving the White House, Mrs. Ford publicly described her struggle with addiction to alcohol and pain medication, and she founded the Betty Ford Clinic for substance abuse in Rancho Mirage, California.

Rosalynn Carter

When Jimmy Carter was president, his wife Rosalynn served as his most trusted advisor and represented him officially during a trip to Central and South American countries. She sometimes sat in on cabinet meetings, where she quietly took notes. These acts aroused much criticism, but there were also those who admired her. Rosalynn's own agenda included supporting mental health reform, actively supporting legislation to reform Social Security, and urging approval of the Equal Rights Amendment. A woman of action, Rosalynn believed firmly in the necessity of women pursuing careers outside the home.

Power of Women (cont.)

Equal Rights Amendment

In 1921, Alice Paul, a suffragist who fought for women's right to vote, wrote the first Equal Rights Amendment (ERA). By 1921, women had gained the right to vote when the 19th Amendment to the Constitution was passed and ratified by the states. However, the right to vote did not guarantee equality of treatment for women. The ERA had been introduced to Congress from 1923-1972, during every session, to make the treatment of women equal to the treatment of men in all areas. It was not until 1972 that the ERA was passed by both houses of Congress.

The ERA that passed in 1972 had three parts: equal rights would not be denied on the basis of sex; Congress would have the power to enforce this provision by appropriate legislation; and the amendment would take effect two years after the date of ratification. Ratification required that ⅔, or 38 states, vote yes to the addition of the amendment to the Constitution.

There was much controversy over the ERA involving both men and women. By July 1982, only 35 states had ratified the amendment; 38 were needed for it to become the 27th Amendment to the Constitution. By that date, the time-limit requirement had lapsed and it was not added. It was reintroduced to Congress again, but did not pass.

The National Organization of Women and many other organizations continued to seek passage of the amendment. Although the ERA was never made a permanent part of the Constitution, its main focus has greatly impacted the legislation passed by Congress on the national level and upon many state laws. Many federal and state laws have been passed requiring that equal treatment be given to women, giving them the same opportunities as men.

During the late 1980s and 1990s, the focus of the ERA was expanded. The amendment being proposed would state that no person may be discriminated against because of "sex, race, sexual orientation, marital status, ethnicity, national origin, color or indigence, age, or disability." This amendment is called the CEA, the Constitutional Equality Amendment.

Power of Women *(cont.)*

Equal Rights Amendment *(cont.)*

Federal laws have been passed that make discrimination against anyone based on these categories to be illegal. Companies, organizations, and institutions that receive federal funds must abide by these laws. For example, the Education Amendment Act of 1972 forbade educational institutions that received federal funds from discriminating on the basis of sex. If a school district needed to hire a new principal, the district could not eliminate candidates because they were women. Today, discrimination on the basis of race, age, or any of the other categories is illegal. If an institution that receives federal funds is found to be discriminatory, it can have its funds revoked. Proponents, people who support the CEA, believe an amendment to the Constitution is still necessary. The Constitution does not clearly identify who, besides males, is to be treated fairly and with equal opportunities. Many people believe that permanent equality for all will not exist unless the Constitution requires it. The legislation that has been passed could be reversed if the Constitution does not mandate equality for all.

Power of Women *(cont.)*

A. Choose a term to describe each first lady of the 1970s. Give an example of something she did to support your choice of trait. Complete the chart below.

First Lady	Characteristic	Supporting Detail

B. Each of the first ladies of the 1970s supported issues she thought were important concerns for Americans. Which causes did each first lady support?

_____

_____

_____

_____

_____

_____

_____

_____

_____

_____

Power of Women *(cont.)*

C. What impact did the Equal Rights Amendment have on society?

_____

_____

_____

_____

_____

_____

_____

_____

_____

_____

Planning Section

Use the space below to plan your response to the essay question that appears on the following page. You may use a graphic organizer or web to help you plan your essay. Write your final essay on the lines provided below the essay question.

Power of Women *(cont.)*

Essay

Why would wives of the presidents of the United States be supportive of the Equal Rights Amendment? Choose one of the first ladies of the 1970s and explain how and why she supported this amendment. Use information from both reading selections.

In your response, be sure to include:

★ an explanation of the Equal Rights Amendment

★ the name of the first lady and her reasons for supporting the amendment

★ what the amendment contains today

Check your essay for proper spelling, grammar, and punctuation.

_____

_____

_____

_____

_____

_____

_____

_____

_____

_____

_____

_____

_____

Marine Disasters

Read the articles entitled "The Unsinkable *Titanic*" and "The *Lusitania*." Both articles are about famous ocean liners that sailed the Atlantic Ocean during the early part of the twentieth century.

You will complete a chart and answer two short-response questions after reading the selections. Then you will write an essay about the two articles. You may look back at the articles as often as necessary.

The Unsinkable *Titanic*

In April of 1912, approximately 2,200 passengers and crew members boarded the *Titanic*, a new luxury liner ready for its maiden voyage. The *Titanic* had the best of everything, and only the elite could afford passage. Some even paid more than $4,000 for the trip, while many of the crew did not even earn $1,000 in a year. The ship's promoters claimed that their vessel was unsinkable, primarily because its hull had 16 watertight compartments. Even if two compartments flooded, the ship would still float. Everyone had confidence in the boat.

A number of famous people were on board, including millionaire John Jacob Astor and his wife, as well as Isidor and Ida Strauss, the wealthy department store owners. In general, the passengers had complete confidence in the ship because the best design and latest technology were at their fingertips.

Late on the night of April 14, the *Titanic* was sailing in the North Atlantic Ocean on its trip from Southampton, England, to New York City. The ship was traveling at a speed of 21 knots (nautical miles per hour), nearly top speed. Since there was danger of icebergs in the area, the ship's speed was dangerously fast. At 11:40 P.M., the *Titanic* rubbed alongside an iceberg for approximately 10 seconds. That was enough! The hull of the ship was made of a type of steel that became brittle in the icy waters of the North Atlantic. Several small cracks appeared instantly, and seams unriveted. Water started to pour inside, weakening the hull even more. Six distress signals were sent out immediately.

Marine Disasters (cont.)

The Unsinkable Titanic (cont.)

Another passenger ship, the *California*, was just 20 minutes away at the time; however, its radio operator was not on duty, so no one there heard the *Titanic's* signal. Another ship, the *Carpathia*, was approximately four hours away, and it responded to the signal. However, when the *Carpathia* arrived at 4:00 A.M., it was too late for many of the passengers: the *Titanic* had long since sunk. Just after 2:00 A.M., water had flooded through the hull to the ship's bow, causing the entire vessel to split in two.

At first, the passengers aboard the ship were calm, expecting to reach lifeboats with ease and then be rescued by other ships. They did not know that the *Titanic's* lifeboats only had room for about 1,200 people, far less than the number of people on board. When the passengers and crew saw how dire the situation was, many stepped aside for younger passengers to board lifeboats safely. Captain Edward J. Smith went down with his ship. In all, 705 people survived the wreck, most of them women and children. The remaining 1,517 died in the icy waters of the North Atlantic Ocean.

In 1985, a team of scientists found the wreckage of the *Titanic* 12,500 feet (3,800 meters) beneath the surface of the sea. Although people had previously thought that a large gash was immediately ripped in the boat because of the iceberg, the scientists were able to prove that the steel composition of the hull was truly the fatal flaw, as was the speed at which the boat was traveling.

The Lusitania

On Saturday, May 1, 1915, the British passenger liner *Lusitania* set sail from Pier 54 in New York, headed for Liverpool, England. On board were 702 crewmembers; 1,257 passengers, and the captain, William Thomas Turner. Of the passengers, 159 were Americans and 168 were infants and children.

On board the *Lusitania* was the typical cargo carried on an ocean liner. Since the *Lusitania* was the largest passenger ship in the world, it could carry a great deal. Perhaps that is why it also carried something extra: 4,200 cases of small-caliber cartridges and other munitions.

The trip across the Atlantic was uneventful, despite the fact that New York reporters had called this the "Last Voyage of the *Lusitania*." War had begun nine months before among Britain, Germany, and many other nations. There were rumors that the Germans, in their new submarines called U-boats (short for *Unterseeboot*), were likely to torpedo any enemy ship. This was, in fact, quite true. German officers had orders to sink all ships because any ship might be carrying supplies to Britain.

The *Lusitania* *(cont.)*

Even passenger ships might hold food for enemy soldiers, and the Germans wished to stop any advantage. In recent weeks, they had torpedoed hundreds of merchant ships in these waters.

On Friday, May 7, the *Lusitania* neared the Irish coast, and everyone was relieved to think they had sailed the ocean without incident. However, it was troubling to discover that the waters were empty. Irish ships were scheduled to escort the *Lusitania* into shore, but they were nowhere to be found. Instead, a torpedo came hurtling through the water, fired from below the surface by a German U-boat. It tore a hole in the *Lusitania*, causing it to list drastically. Many people were killed instantly. Others tried to board and release the lifeboats. The listing ship tipped back and forth, causing the lifeboats to crash against its sides. Hundreds of evacuees were thrown into the water. In 18 minutes, the *Lusitania*—which was supposed to be unsinkable—had sunk. The captain stayed until the end, eventually clinging to a floating chair for safety. The survivors of the attack held pieces of wood and other buoyant objects to keep themselves afloat. Six of the original 48 lifeboats made it safely into the water.

In all, more than 1,200 people died. Children and infants comprised about 10% of that number, and Americans accounted for 128 of the dead.

President Woodrow Wilson made a formal protest to the German government, which issued an apology for the error. However, many Americans were outraged, as were nations around the world. The sinking of the *Lusitania* became a rallying cry for troops everywhere, and eventually it became one of the catalysts for America's entry into the Great War, World War I.

Marine Disasters *(cont.)*

A. Complete the chart comparing the facts about the two sailing vessels.

Main Ideas	*Titanic*	*Lusitania*
Departure Point/Date		
Destination		
Number of Passengers/Crew		
Death Toll		
Cause of Destruction		

B. Why weren't the people on board the *Titanic* rescued before the ship sank?

_____

_____

_____

_____

_____

_____

_____

_____

_____

_____

Marine Disasters *(cont.)*

C. Why do you think the sinking of the *Lusitania* is considered to be one of the reasons that caused America to become involved in World War I?

_____

_____

_____

_____

_____

_____

_____

_____

_____

_____

Planning Section

Use the space below to plan your response to the essay question that appears on the following page. You may use a graphic organizer or web to help you plan your essay. Write your final essay on the lines provided below the essay question.

Marine Disasters *(cont.)*

Essay

Write an essay comparing the two ocean liners (the *Titanic* and the *Lusitania*) that were claimed to be unsinkable. Use information from both reading selections.

In your response, be sure to include:

★ how the ships were similar

★ how the ships were different

★ how each ship was destroyed

★ how each ship had an impact on history

Check your essay for proper spelling, grammar, and punctuation.

_____

_____

_____

_____

_____

_____

_____

_____

_____

_____

_____

_____

Freedom Rings

Read the articles entitled "Symbols of Freedom" and "Flags Are Flying." These articles discuss objects that represent the various types of freedoms that exist for humankind.

You will complete a chart and answer two short-response questions about the reading selections. Then you will write an essay about the articles. You may look back at the articles as often as necessary.

Symbols of Freedom

Freedom in its purest form is the absolute ability to make choices for oneself without restriction and with the ample provision of all supporting information, time, and conditions. But no formal society, no matter how supportive that society is of personal freedoms, allows freedom to exist without limitations. In a free society like the United States, no person is allowed absolute freedom. Rules and laws exist to protect the freedoms of everyone.

There are various kinds of freedom—for example, intellectual, physical, political, social, and personal. Intellectual freedom is the opportunity to think and learn without restriction. Physical freedom is the limitless opportunity to move. When one is physically free, one can come and go as one pleases, whenever one pleases. There are no restrictions to movement. Political freedom is the opportunity for all people to take part in the governmental decision-making process. Politically free people are allowed to express their opinions. Decisions for all the people are voted on by all the people. Social freedom is the opportunity to live, worship, speak, work, and interrelate as one chooses. Each person has the right to be exactly who he or she is. Personal freedom provides the unrestricted space and leisure to know oneself. This freedom allows each person to learn and grow, to develop into who he or she really is or can become. It suggests personal peace.

Freedom Rings *(cont.)*

Symbols of Freedom *(cont.)*

Light

A common symbol for intellectual freedom is light. Often when protesters are rallying for a certain cause, they will hold single candles, symbolizing the need for enlightenment. It is their wish that the minds of society will open up to receive their cause, and that all people will join together in support of it. A light bulb is also used as a symbol for intellectual freedom. When it shines, it symbolizes that a person has recognized an idea or a thought.

Golden Gate Bridge

The Golden Gate Bridge is a beautiful and majestic symbol of freedom that has stood at the entrance to the San Francisco Bay since 1937. The bridge is a symbol of freedom because, like any bridge, it opens up possibilities for travel that were once restricted and even impossible. The bridge also serves as a reminder of the limitless capabilities of human ingenuity, being one of the largest, most encompassing, and most spectacular suspension bridges ever built.

The architectural design of the Golden Gate Bridge is truly masterful. It is 4,200 feet (1,280 meters) long and 90 feet (27 meters) wide. It rises 220 feet (67 meters) above the Pacific Ocean. Six lanes of traffic plus a sidewalk on either side run the length of the bridge. No wonder the bridge cost 35.5 million dollars to build!

Freedom Rings *(cont.)*

Symbols of Freedom *(cont.)*

Victory Gardens

During World War II, there was a great rush of patriotic fervor in the United States. People rallied around the causes of the war and did everything they could to help the war effort. Victory Gardens became a common sight. The Victory Garden was an attempt to help in the war effort by producing more food. Troops overseas needed to be fed, and food at home was being rationed (allotted sparingly). People grew vegetables in any garden space they could find in order to supplement both. The Victory Garden has come to symbolize an individual's support of the causes of his or her government, a symbol of political freedom.

Doves

The white dove is a bird that has come to symbolize peace. White is the traditional color of purity and goodness. Peace is the ultimate goal of a nation and its people. A peaceful nation would be more apt to provide its people with social freedoms so that people can live as they wish.

Birds

Birds are traditional symbols for personal freedom. Their ability to fly is enviable to the land-bound human being, for birds carry within them the means to absolute liberty. We have searched for centuries to discover a way to copy their freedom of movement and make it our own. In recent history we have experienced some success. Even so, the innate ability of birds is beyond us, and we can only yearn to "try our wings" as birds do.

Freedom Rings *(cont.)*

Flags Are Flying

Nations, states, provinces, and private organizations around the world have adopted flags to show reverence and respect for that which they symbolize. Shown below are some flags and their meanings.

Argentina

The stripes are blue and white, depicting the colors worn by the soldiers who fought the British in 1806–1807. The yellow sun represents the country's freedom from Spain.

Canada

The red and white flag features a red maple leaf with 11 points. It is the national symbol for Canada.

China

This flag is red with yellow stars. The large star designates the leadership of the communists. The smaller stars depict groups of workers.

Greece

The blue of the flag represents the sky and the sea. The white represents the purity of Greece's fight for independence. The white cross stands for the Greek Orthodox religion.

The Red Cross

The red cross on this white flag is a literal representation of the organization's name. It is also a tribute to Switzerland, where the Red Cross was founded. (The Swiss flag shows a white cross on a red background.) This same organization has slightly different flags depending on the nation in which it is located. For example, in Israel the flag shows a red Star of David on a white field, and in Muslim countries there is a red crescent centered on a white background.

Freedom Rings *(cont.)*

A. There are various types of freedoms. Identify three types of freedoms and objects that traditionally symbolize that particular freedom.

Type of Freedom	Symbol

B. What was the purpose of the Victory Gardens?

_____

_____

_____

_____

_____

_____

_____

_____

Freedom Rings *(cont.)*

C. Why is the Golden Gate Bridge a symbol of freedom?

Use details to support your answer.

_____

_____

_____

_____

_____

_____

_____

_____

_____

_____

Planning Section

Use the space below to plan your response to the essay question that appears on the following page. You may use a graphic organizer or web to help you plan your essay. Write your final essay on the lines provided below the essay question.

Freedom Rings *(cont.)*

Essay

Symbols are objects that represent ideas. One major symbol recognized worldwide is a flag. Flags are used to represent nations, organizations, and even small groups. How is a flag designed? Choose 2–3 flags from the article to support your essay.

In your essay, be sure to include:

★ an introductory paragraph

★ supporting details and examples

★ a concluding sentence or paragraph

Check your essay for proper spelling, grammar, and punctuation.

_____

_____

_____

_____

_____

_____

_____

_____

_____

_____

_____

_____

The Great World Wars

You are going to read two articles. The first article is about a war that was fought on three continents and lasted from 1914 through 1918. It was known simply as the Great War. When a second war was begun in the '30s, the Great War's name was changed to World War I. The second article is about the second world war named World War II. The United States' involvement began in 1941 and lasted for four years.

First you will complete a chart and two short-response questions. Then you will write an essay about the two articles. You may look back at the articles as often as necessary.

"The Great War"—World War I

The assassinations of Archduke Ferdinand and his wife, Sophie, in June 1914, began the war, which included the Allied Powers (Russia, Great Britain, France) and the Central Powers (Germany and Austria-Hungary). Italy entered the war in 1915. The conflict eventually involved the vital sea routes and oil fields of the Middle East. In February 1917, German U-boats were ordered to sink all ships bound for British harbors. Five American ships were sunk, and the United States' involvement in the war seemed inevitable. War was declared on April 6, 1917. Men were quickly drafted and sent to help the Royal Navy hunt down the German U-boats. The U.S. troops under General Pershing proved to be a decisive factor in the victory of the Allied forces.

After several defeats, General Ludendorff felt that Germany could not win the war. He advised his countrymen to try to make peace with the Italian, French, British, and American forces. The war drew to a rapid close. In Germany, revolutionaries took over the government, and an armistice was signed on November 11, 1918.

The Treaty of Versailles, signed June 28, 1919, established the independent countries of Poland, Czechoslovakia, and Yugoslavia. It also set up the League of Nations where countries could settle disputes in peace. Germany was excluded from the League of Nations and became increasingly hostile. Twenty-one years later, the world entered another horrible war in which Germany was again a major participant.

The Great World Wars *(cont.)*

World War II

America entered World War II after the Japanese bombed Pearl Harbor on December 7, 1941. All men between the ages of 21 and 35 had to register for the draft. Women worked factory jobs related to and in support of the war effort.

The Allies—Great Britain, the United States, and the U.S.S.R.—were at war with the Axis Powers—Germany, Italy, and Japan.

Adolf Hitler, Germany's leader, had already occupied Poland, Belgium, Luxembourg, Holland, and France when the Americans came ashore at Normandy, France. This D-Day invasion at Normandy was led by a general named Dwight Eisenhower.

From Normandy, the Allies swept through France and into Belgium, Holland, and Luxembourg. The Americans fought back the Germans during the Battle of the Bulge at the borders of Belgium and Luxembourg.

In the Pacific, General Douglas MacArthur prepared to retake the Philippine Islands. The Japanese suffered great casualties and lost many ships and aircraft, but they were not easily conquered. America could tell that Germany was collapsing, and they did not want the war to continue indefinitely. It was decided that an atomic bomb would be dropped on the Japanese city of Hiroshima. When that action failed to produce Japan's surrender, a second atomic bomb was dropped—this time on Nagasaki. This marked the end of the war.

At the conclusion of World War II, both freedom and democracy had been preserved. The United States emerged as a leading world power and was involved with the peace settlements and aid to countries damaged by the war. The U.S.S.R. also emerged as a leading world power. Germany was divided and ruled by several world powers. Its wartime leadership was brought to trial in front of the world. Japan, devastated, had to rebuild its cities and economy. Italy, France, Great Britain, and other European nations needed aid, as well, in order to reestablish themselves.

The Great World Wars *(cont.)*

A. To fill out this diagram, use the countries involved in the "Great War," as well as the cause and results at the end of the war.

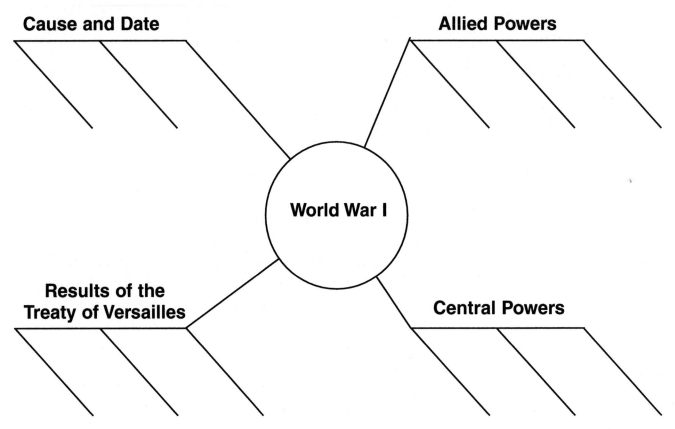

Cause and Date

Allied Powers

World War I

Results of the Treaty of Versailles

Central Powers

B. The Treaty of Versailles had both positive and negative results. Using examples from the selection, explain why this statement is true.

_____

_____

_____

_____

_____

_____

_____

_____

_____

The Great World Wars *(cont.)*

C. Explain the results the bombing of Pearl Harbor had on people in America.

_____

_____

_____

_____

_____

_____

_____

_____

_____

_____

Planning Section

Use the space below to plan your response to the essay question that appears on the following page. You may use a graphic organizer or web to help you plan your essay. Write your final essay on the lines provided below the essay question.

The Great World Wars *(cont.)*

Essay

World War I and World War II changed the world. Explain why this statement is true. In your essay:

★ name one change brought about by each of the two World Wars

★ explain the effects these changes had on the world

★ explain why these were positive or negative changes

Be sure to check your essay for correct grammar, punctuation, and spelling.

_____

_____

_____

_____

_____

_____

_____

_____

_____

_____

_____

_____

_____

_____

Decades of Change

You are going to read two articles about periods of time in American history when great changes were taking place. "The Roaring Twenties" was a decade in which great self-expression and economic prosperity existed in the U.S. The second article, "The Great Depression," is about the 10-year period following The Roaring Twenties.

First, you will complete a chart and two short-response questions. Then you will write an essay about the two articles. You may look back at the articles as often as necessary.

The Roaring Twenties

In the Twenties, the country entered an era of prosperity. World War I had ended and the United States had been among the victors. Confident feelings ran high as the soldiers returned home. They were eager to enjoy themselves and live life to the fullest. Fostered by presidents who favored business, the stock market reached new heights. These feelings and attitudes contributed to the social changes that followed.

Prohibition, or the outlawing of the consumption of all alcoholic beverages, became the law in 1920. Despite the enactment of the law, prohibition was largely ignored. In fact, drinking became commonplace among women and youth: it became a new symbol of defiance. People made their own version of alcohol in their homes, called "bathtub gin." Prohibition also gave rise to organized crime and increased violence. Mobsters, like Al Capone, supplied illegal alcohol across the country to customers who gathered to drink in secret saloons called "speakeasies." By 1933, there were more than 200,000 speakeasies throughout the United States.

Entertainment gained new importance for Americans. About half of America's homes had electricity, primarily used for lighting. Radio brought nightly comedy shows and news to families throughout the country. Television was introduced to the public in 1928.

Decades of Change *(cont.)*

The Roaring Twenties *(cont.)*

By the end of the twenties, many families had automobiles, a novelty at the beginning of the decade. Trains remained a favorite mode of long distance travel. Charles Lindbergh's solo flight across the Atlantic Ocean on May 20, 1927, was celebrated with the decade's largest ticker-tape parade, held in New York City on June 11, 1927. Audiences in 1927 were excited to see the first talking movie, *The Jazz Singer*, and they cheered as Babe Ruth hit 60 home runs. In 1928, Walt Disney produced the first cartoon, *Steamboat Willie*. Women bobbed (or cut) their hair, smoked cigarettes, and wore short skirts. The Charleston was the popular dance craze.

Composers George Gershwin and Aaron Copland, writers Ernest Hemingway and F. Scott Fitzgerald, and artists Mary Cassatt and Grant Wood became prominent. In the predominately black section of Harlem (in New York City), the Harlem Renaissance produced a host of great African-American writers, artists, and musicians. Harlem's popular night spot, The Cotton Club, drew people who enjoyed dance and musical entertainment.

Decades of Change (cont.)

The Great Depression

In an effort to get rich quick, people invested heavily in the stock market. When President Coolidge left office, he declared that the market was sound.

On Tuesday, October 29, 1929, the stock market collapsed. Ten billion dollars in stock were lost in very heavy trading in only a few hours that day. Stocks that had sold for $20–$40 a share just a few weeks before now sold for pennies. High rollers who had been speculating in the market were immediately bankrupted.

President Hoover's claim that the country's business was "on sound and prosperous basis" proved to be tragically incorrect. In the weeks and months that followed, the effects were even more profound. Five thousand banks failed and closed their doors, causing over nine million people to lose their savings accounts. Banks failed because they had heavily invested in the stock market. The country was thrown into economic chaos.

For the first three years following the stock market crash, an average of 100,000 jobs were lost each week. Since so many people were out of work or in danger of losing their jobs, people began to economize and avoid unnecessary purchases. As demand for goods decreased, businesses were forced to lay off workers, adding to unemployment. There was no government welfare at the time.

Soon people's money ran out and they were unable to pay their mortgages and other debts. They lost their homes, cars, and other valuables. Hardship became a way of life. Some families were forced to beg or wait on breadlines for food. They lived in shacks made of discarded lumber and cardboard. These shanty towns sprang up in big cities. The towns became known as "Hoovervilles," after President Hoover, and the newspapers they used for blankets were called "Hoover blankets." In 1932, one out of four Americans was unemployed. President Hoover firmly believed that government should stay out of business and refused to offer any help until 1932. Billions of dollars were loaned to failing business under the Reconstruction Finance Corporation Bill.

Decades of Change *(cont.)*

The Great Depression *(cont.)*

Farmers were unprepared for the drought on the Great Plains that turned the rich topsoil into useless desert. Cattle choked on the dust. There was nothing for farmers to do but pack up and move west, hoping for work in the fields of California. The life of a migrant worker was created. Later, movements for the formation of unions began. Unions used tactics such as strikes and sit-ins to gain better pay and working conditions.

When Franklin Delano Roosevelt was elected president of the United States in 1932, he enacted his program called "The New Deal." He closed all banks so federal auditors could examine their records. Financially sound banks were allowed to reopen. On March 31, 1933, the Civilian Conservation Corps provided jobs for nearly three million young men. More helpful legislation followed to help the economy recover.

Radio dominated American life. Through his "fireside chats," President Roosevelt explained his politics and reassured America that the economy would recover. Programs such as "The Lone Ranger" and "Amos 'n' Andy" helped people forget their troubles. At the movies, Bugs Bunny and Porky Pig debuted, helping people to laugh. Double features, two movies for the price of one, helped people economize on entertainment. Child star Shirley Temple charmed audiences with her singing and dancing—even President Roosevelt acknowledged the tiny actor's contribution.

At the end of the 1930s, focus shifted overseas to the rise of fascism in Germany, Italy, and Japan. With war beginning in 1939, America would be swept into a new era of history.

Decades of Change *(cont.)*

A. Compare the Roaring Twenties and the Great Depression in terms of economy, homes, and jobs.

The Roaring Twenties		The Great Depression
	Economy	
	Homes	
	Jobs	

B. The writer feels that "The Roaring Twenties" was a time of great opportunity. Use at least two details from the selection to prove that his belief was correct.

_____

_____

_____

_____

_____

_____

_____

_____

_____

Decades of Change *(cont.)*

C. Why are the years 1929 to 1939 called the Great Depression? Use three examples from the selection to illustrate the impact those years had on the economy in America.

_____

_____

_____

_____

_____

_____

_____

_____

_____

Planning Section

Use the space below to plan your response to the essay question that appears on the following page. You may use a graphic organizer or web to help you plan your essay. Write your final essay on the lines provided below the essay question.

Decades of Change *(cont.)*

Essay

Both the Roaring Twenties and the Great Depression were times of great change. Write a journal entry telling about a conversation your family might have had about their plans for the coming week during the 1930s.

In your response be sure to include:

★ where they would be living

★ examples of their hopes for the future

★ what friends and relatives were doing

Check your essay for correct grammar, punctuation, and spelling.

_____

_____

_____

_____

_____

_____

_____

_____

_____

_____

_____

_____

Documenting Through Photography

Read the article entitled "Failing Farmers" and the biographical sketch about Dorothea Lange. "Failing Farmers" discusses the plight of farmers during the 1930s. The article "Dorothea Lange" chronicles the accomplishments of this famous photographer.

First, you will complete a chart and the two short-response questions. Then you will write an essay about the two articles. You may look back at the articles as often as necessary.

Failing Farmers

Farmers did not share in the prosperity of World War I, and things grew worse after the recession of 1921. Federal support for agriculture ended and many farmers who had expanded their production to meet wartime needs lost their land and stock. For those who survived, low crop prices meant low income. In the 1930s wheat prices dropped to below what it cost to grow the crop. Rather than sell at such prices, some farmers destroyed their own crops. A series of natural disasters made matters even worse and led to the greatest westward migration that the United States has ever seen.

Americans had long disregarded the warnings of conservationists. Farmers had misused the land, depleting fertile soil and then moving on to farm new land. In the Great Plains, farmers plowed up natural grasses to plant wheat. Agriculturists advised the use of contour plowing to prevent erosion. They also suggested planting trees as windbreakers. Both suggestions were ignored by the farmers. When a seven-year drought struck, beginning in 1931, winds blew the topsoil into thick, dark clouds of dust that sometimes lasted for several days. To protect themselves from the dust storms, farmers hung damp sheets over the windows of their homes. Still, dust poured through the cracks of the farmhouse walls, leaving dust in their food, hair, eyes, mouth, and pockets. For many, there was nothing left to do but leave their farms and head west.

Documenting Through Photography *(cont.)*

Failing Farmers *(cont.)*

Over three million people eventually migrated from the Great Plains region to California, where there was the promise of jobs. However, conditions in California proved to be not much better than the farms that they had left. While there was not much dust to contend with, there were not nearly enough jobs. Californians resented these new people and labeled them "Okies," a synonym for dumb and lazy. Hatred against them was so great that some farmers destroyed their surplus food rather than share it with the starving Okie families.

Finally, the government stepped in and created some labor camps in the San Joaquin Valley, which provided relief and education for the migrants. Much was written about these people and their struggles. John Steinbeck's novel *The Grapes of Wrath* described conditions among the Okies in California. Dorothea Lange photographed and documented their misery, while Woody Guthrie sang songs about their predicament.

John Steinbeck

Woody Guthrie

Documenting Through Photography *(cont.)*

Dorothea Lange

Artists do not always use paints, brushes, and easels. One woman used a camera and film to record what she saw. Her pictures helped to change lives.

Dorothea Lange was born in New Jersey in 1895. Her childhood was not easy. Dorothea's father left his family when she was just a child. At the age of seven, she had polio, which left her with a limp. Dorothea caused some of her own problems because she often skipped school. She spent those days wandering through the city and making notes about what she saw. By the time she was 18, she knew that she wanted to use a camera to record the things she saw.

Dorothea went to California and set up a studio. She continued to be interested in everything she saw and could now record it on film. Her photographs told of the unemployment, hunger, and despair of the 1920s and the 1930s.

Even though her photographs were not always appealing to others, Dorothea exhibited them in 1934. Paul Taylor, a sociologist and economist, was impressed with her work. The two began to document the living conditions of the migrant worker on film for books, magazine articles, and exhibits. Their impact was great! Americans demanded improvements in the lives of migrants as a result of the work of this team, who later married.

Documenting Through Photography *(cont.)*

Dorothea Lange *(cont.)*

During the 1930s, Dorothea became a full-time photographer for the Farm Security Administration. She recorded the erosion of the soil and the lives of the people in the Dust Bowl. In the early 1940s, she was hired by the War Relocation Authority. Her task was to document the lives of Japanese aliens and the Japanese-Americans who were forced by the United States government to live in camps. Because her photographs showed the difficult life of these prisoners, many of her photographs were not released until after the war. Her next project, photographing the United Nations Conference of 1945, had to be stopped when Dorothea became ill. Her illness lasted several years.

By 1951, Dorothea was able to work again. Her photographs began to focus on family life. Several of her assignments were for *Life* magazine. In 1964, Dorothea found she had cancer, but she did not stop her work. She designed an exhibit of her photographs, planned a center for documentary photography, and recorded a study of the country women of America. Dorothea died in 1965, but her photographs remain. They remind us of how she helped others by depicting their conditions.

Documenting Through Photography *(cont.)*

A. Complete the timeline chart by listing the important events in Dorothea Lange's life that correspond to the years listed.

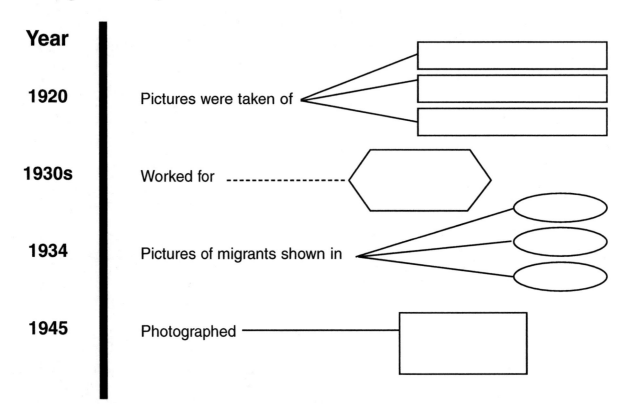

Year

1920   Pictures were taken of

1930s   Worked for ---------------------

1934   Pictures of migrants shown in

1945   Photographed

B. What emotions might Dorothea Lange's photographs evoke from viewers? Use details from the story to support your answer.

_____

_____

_____

_____

_____

_____

_____

_____

Documenting Through Photography *(cont.)*

C. How did nature and the negligence of farmers contribute to the problems that the farmers of the Dust Bowl faced? Use specific examples from the story.

_____

_____

_____

_____

_____

_____

_____

_____

Planning Section

Use the space below to plan your response to the essay question that appears on the following page. You may use a graphic organizer or web to help you plan your essay. Write your final essay on the lines provided below the essay question.

Documenting Through Photography *(cont.)*

Essay

The times in which Dorothea Lange lived and the time of the Dust Bowl were periods of great difficulty and social change. Do you think that there are important events and conditions that should be or are being documented today?

In your response, be sure to include:

★ the problems that existed in the past that contributed to human hardship

★ how society in the 1930s reacted to these problems

★ how you feel the problems of today compare to those of the 1930s and how people in society today would react

Check your essay for proper spelling, grammar, and punctuation.

_____

_____

_____

_____

_____

_____

_____

_____

_____

_____

_____

_____

Ancient Greek Heroes

Read the Greek myths entitled "Helen of Troy" and "Hercules." Each myth demonstrates the importance of heroic efforts, strength, and beauty to the people of ancient Greece. Greek myths were the center of ancient Greek culture and religion. They explained both natural and historical events, as well as elements of human nature for Greek people.

You will complete a chart and answer two short-response questions about the reading selections. Then you will write an essay about the two articles. You may look back at the articles as often as necessary.

Helen of Troy

It is uncertain as to whether Helen was a real person or part of a myth created to explain the Trojan War. It is said that Helen's father was the god Zeus and her mother was Leda of Sparta.

Stories about Helen's beauty were told throughout the land. Princes from all over Greece came to court her. Finally, she decided to marry Menelaus, who was the king of Sparta. Helen and Menelaus were happily married until they had a visit from Paris, who was a Trojan prince. Paris had come to see if Helen was as beautiful as he had heard. Helen's beauty was breathtaking and he became obsessed by this. Paris kidnapped Helen and took her back to Troy with him. When Menelaus found out that Paris had taken his beautiful wife, he became enraged.

Menelaus asked the Greek warriors to help him go to war against Troy and retrieve his wife. Many warriors wanted to help the king, so they boarded their ships and sailed to Troy, which was located in Asia Minor. The Greeks expected to celebrate a quick victory over the Trojans. However, they were never able to break through the walls around Troy. The Greeks and Trojans fought for 10 years before there was an end to the bloodshed. Some say that Helen spent all those years in the Trojan castle weaving a tapestry that would tell her sad story.

Finally, a man named Odysseus thought of a clever plan to defeat the Trojans and rescue Helen. He secretly built a large wooden horse. Fifty soldiers hid inside of it. The remaining Greeks moved the horse next to the city walls so it could be seen by the Trojans. Then they left and appeared to sail away. The Trojans were curious about this huge, wooden horse so they took it inside their city walls. When it was nightfall, the Greek soldiers came out of the horse and defeated the Trojans. The beautiful Helen of Troy was returned to her husband, Menelaus.

Ancient Greek Heroes *(cont.)*

Hercules

Hercules is a great hero in Greek mythology. He was the son of Zeus, king of the gods of Olympus, and a mortal woman named Alcmena. He was born in the ancient Greek city of Thebes.

When Hercules was just a baby, he began showing that he had great strength by killing two serpents, or snakes, who were about to attack him. As he grew up, he became famous for his strength and his kindness to those in need. He learned wrestling, archery, and fencing. Although Hercules was basically a good person, he had one serious problem: he had a terrible temper. His temper was so uncontrollable that he had been banished from Thebes. Hercules was told that the only way he could make up for his behavior was to serve King Eurystheus of Argolis for 12 years. During this time, Hercules was given many difficult tasks to accomplish, but he was determined to do them all.

Hercules was required to complete 12 very difficult labors, or tasks. First, Hercules had to go to Nemea and kill a fierce lion that lived there. Hercules wore the lion's skin to show that he was successful. Second, he had to kill a horrible serpent called the Hydra of Lerna. The hydra had several heads, which could grow back if they were cut off. Hercules found a way to keep the heads from growing back and was able to defeat the hydra. His third feat was to capture the Arcadian stag with golden horns. Then the fourth thing Hercules had to do was to catch the huge boar of Erymanthus. The fifth task required Hercules to go to Lake Stymphalus and scare some vicious birds away from the woods there. Then Hercules used two rivers to clean the king's stables. Hercules had to go to Crete to complete the next task. There he had to capture the bull that belonged to King Minos. For his eighth task, Hercules had to bring human-eating horses from King Diomedes of Thrace to his king. Hercules had to defeat the queen of the Amazons for his ninth task. The last three tasks made Hercules immortal: he had to take cattle away from the monster Geryon, steal Golden Apples from the Tree of Life, and catch a three-headed watchdog named Cerberus. The Greeks greatly admired physical strength and beauty, as well as intelligence. Hercules embodied these characteristics and is a prime example of a Greek hero.

Ancient Greek Heroes *(cont.)*

A. Choose three terms that describe Hercules. Give supporting details that illustrate each characteristic.

Characteristic	Supporting Details

B. Which of the 12 tasks do you think would be most difficult? Explain your answer.

_____

_____

_____

_____

_____

_____

_____

_____

_____

_____

_____

Ancient Greek Heroes *(cont.)*

C. How did the Greeks defeat the Trojans?

_____

_____

_____

_____

_____

_____

_____

_____

_____

Planning Section

Use the space below to plan your response to the essay question that appears on the following page. You may use a graphic organizer or web to help you plan your essay. Write your final essay on the lines provided below the essay question.

Ancient Greek Heroes *(cont.)*

Essay

The myths of Ancient Greece reflected the Greeks' high regard for human development, mental and physical. They valued intelligence and beautiful faces and bodies. Their heroes were brave, strong, and determined—powerful role models. In addition, Greek heroes, often of mixed parentage—part god and part human, or mortal—had to complete extraordinary tasks. The myths of Hercules and Helen of Troy are typical of Greek myths. In your essay, choose three ways each story is a prime example of Greek myths. Use details from both reading selections.

In your essay, be sure to include:

★ an introductory topic sentence or paragraph

★ supporting details from each selection

★ a concluding sentence or paragraph

Check your essay for proper spelling, grammar, and punctuation.

_____

_____

_____

_____

_____

_____

_____

_____

_____

_____

_____

_____

_____

Courageous Women

Read the excerpt from the novel *Island of the Blue Dolphins* and the article entitled "Women of Courage." The excerpt from *Island of the Blue Dolphins* tells the thoughts of Karana, a young woman who is stranded on a deserted island and must overcome obstacles in order to survive. Karana is a fictional character who exhibits character traits that real people often possess. She endures obstacles in life that modern women often face. "Women of Courage" describes three courageous women who have broken with society's accepted ways and challenged stereotypes (fixed or unchangeable ways of looking at things).

You will complete a chart and answer two short-response questions about the reading selections. Then you will write an essay about the two articles. You may look back at the articles as often as necessary.

Island of the Blue Dolphins

The novel *Island of the Blue Dolphins* is about Karana and her brother, Ramo, who become stranded on a deserted island. When Ramo is killed by a pack of wild dogs, Karana is truly alone. Because the women in her tribe traditionally did not learn many of the tasks related to survival, Karana must depend on her own ingenuity and skills. She performs tasks such as creating weapons to use against wild dogs and other creatures. In addition she somehow survives an earthquake and a tidal wave. Even though she must demonstrate characteristics and skills generally associated with males in order to survive, the consequences of going against tribal tradition worry her:

> *As I lay there, I wondered what would happen to me if I went against the law of our tribe which forbade the making of weapons by women. . . . Would the four winds blow in from the four directions of the world and smother me as I made the weapons? Or would the earth tremble, as many said and bury me beneath the falling rocks? Or, as others said, would the sea rise over the island in a terrible flood?*

Despite her fears, Karana goes against tradition and constructs the weapons and other items she needs to survive.

Courageous Women *(cont.)*

Women of Courage

A woman's place in society has changed drastically over the last century. Traditionally a woman's role has been in the home or only at certain jobs. Three women who have challenged society's stereotypes by entering the workforce in areas generally dominated by males are Elizabeth Blackwell, Sandra Day O'Connor, and Sally Ride. Read on to meet these women of courage.

Dr. Elizabeth Blackwell

"Code Blue! All available medical personnel, please report to the emergency room immediately!" Where once only male doctors would have answered this page, today doctors of both genders answer it. But not long ago, the medical profession had stereotyped roles—men became doctors; women became nurses. When women were finally accepted to and graduated from medical school, they were viewed with suspicion and distrust. It required much courage to tear down the walls of discrimination and prejudice. Today, about half of all students in medical school are women.

Elizabeth Blackwell (1821–1910) was the first woman in the United States to obtain a degree from medical school when she graduated from Geneva Medical School in 1849. Her many accomplishments included the establishment of the New York Infirmary for Women and Children in 1857. She also aided in the founding of the London School of Medicine in England (her native country) in 1869. Because of her groundbreaking achievements in medicine, the Blackwell Medal of Recognition has been awarded annually to outstanding women physicians since 1949.

Sandra Day O'Connor

The Supreme Court, the highest court in our nation, is composed of nine members—one Chief Justice and eight associate justices. The function of the Supreme Court is to help "lower" courts interpret and understand how the laws of our land operate. Supreme Court justices are appointed by the President and approved by Congress.

Women of Courage (cont.)

Also, they are appointed for life. Despite the fact that the Supreme Court has been in existence since the early days of our government's existence, it was not until 1981 that a woman, Sandra Day O'Connor, was nominated. The road to this position for her was a very difficult one.

Justice O'Connor was born in El Paso, Texas on March 26, 1930. Despite graduating with high honors and ranking third in her class at Stanford University, a very prestigious law school, Justice O'Connor had difficulty obtaining a position as a lawyer. When she initially sought employment, Justice O'Connor was offered secretarial work. Her perseverance to excel in her profession demonstrates that she is a courageous woman.

She eventually practiced her chosen profession. She served in the Arizona State Senate from 1972–1974, then became a judge for the Arizona Supreme Court in 1974–1979. She next served on the Arizona Court of Appeals from 1979–1981. Finally, in 1981 she accepted the prestigious position of Supreme Court justice, a position never before held by a woman.

Sally Ride

"Five, four, three, two, one. Ignition! We have a lift off!" This familiar phrase signals that yet another journey into outer space has begun, a thrilling and courageous endeavor. Very few individuals have the courage to become astronauts. One member of this elite group is Sally Kirsten Ride, the first female astronaut. Like Karana in *Island of the Blue Dolphins,* Ride accepted challenges traditionally faced only by men. Her accomplishments mark "one giant step for womankind!"

Ride was born on May 26, 1951. She earned a Ph.D. in physics from Stanford University in 1977, a degree that provided her with the required knowledge to become a member of the flight crew on space shuttle missions in 1983 and 1984. After completing these missions, she headed a 10-member study team formed to map the future goals for 21st-century exploration. Two ideas the team suggested were the establishment of a lunar base and the creation of a strong earth-science study program for astronauts.

Courageous Women *(cont.)*

A. What were the major events in the life of Elizabeth Blackwell?

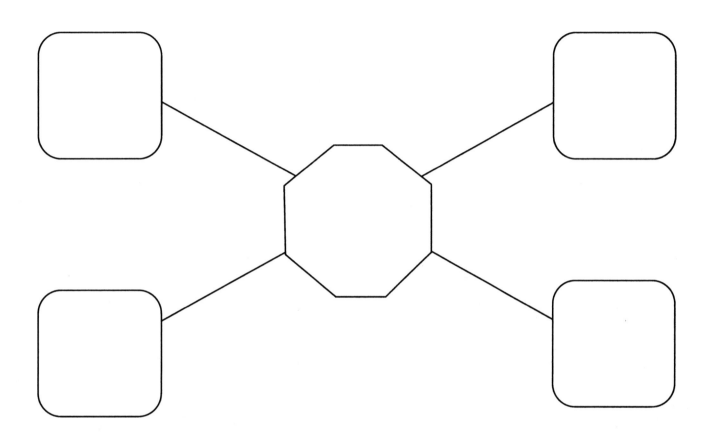

B. What was Karana imagining as she prepared to take steps in order to survive on the island?

_____

_____

_____

_____

_____

_____

Courageous Women *(cont.)*

C. What obstacles did Sandra Day O'Connor have to overcome in reaching for her goals?

_____

_____

_____

_____

_____

_____

_____

_____

Planning Section

Use the space below to plan your response to the essay question that appears on the following page. You may use a graphic organizer or web to help you plan your essay. Write your final essay on the lines provided below the essay question.

Courageous Women *(cont.)*

Essay

For centuries society has set roles and duties for each gender—male and female. What were society's standards and how have they changed during the twentieth century? To support your answer use details from both readings.

In your response, be sure to include:

★ the standards that existed in the past; discriminations women have experienced

★ how society's standards have changed in reality and in fiction

★ how you feel about stereotypes for men and women

Check your essay for proper spelling, grammar, and punctuation.

_____

_____

_____

_____

_____

_____

_____

_____

_____

_____

_____

_____

Art Appreciation

Read the articles entitled "Norman Rockwell" and "Henri Matisse." Both articles are about famous painters of the twentieth century. Norman Rockwell is an American with a very unique style of painting. Henri Matisse was a French painter whose style of painting made him a leader in the art world.

You will complete a chart and answer two short-response questions about the reading selections. Then you will write an essay about the two articles. You may look back at the articles as often as necessary.

Norman Rockwell

For 47 years Norman Rockwell painted covers for the magazine *The Saturday Evening Post*. His inviting paintings provided intimate glimpses into the everyday lives of Americans during the first half of the twentieth century and have come to be regarded as classic Americana. In his realistic paintings and illustrations, Rockwell combined repetition of color and shape to create a specific rhythm and mood that reflected common occurrences in everyday life. He attempted to show the America he knew to others who might not have noticed. According to Rockwell, "Common places never become common. It is we who become tired when we cease to be curious and appreciative."

Norman Rockwell was born on February 3, 1894, in New York. When he was nine, the family moved to Mamaroneck. To gain acceptance, the resourceful Rockwell drew pictures to entertain his classmates. He left high school to study at the National Academy of Design and earned money by drawing greeting cards. At age 16, he studied at the Art Students League and began illustrating books and magazines. By the time he was 18, Rockwell was the art director of *Boys' Life* magazine.

Rockwell achieved fame after the five illustrations he sold to the editor of *The Saturday Evening Post* were used as covers on the magazine. In all, Norman Rockwell provided 318 covers for the Post through his 47-year association with them.

Art Appreciation (cont.)

Norman Rockwell (cont.)

When World War I broke out, Rockwell tried to enlist in the Navy, but he was rejected for being underweight. Undeterred, he ate a diet of bananas and donuts until he gained the necessary 10 pounds. After acceptance in the service, Rockwell was assigned to the navy yard in Charleston, South Carolina where he painted for the Navy. He also continued to work for *The Saturday Evening Post* and other magazines. After the war, he returned to New York where he built a studio for himself. By that time he was enjoying both fame and fortune from his paintings.

The process used by Norman Rockwell to create a painting was long and detailed. First, he sketched the scene. Next he made individual drawings of each element in the scene. Full-sized charcoal drawings were the next step, followed by color sketches. Only then was he ready to begin the actual painting.

In the late 1930s Rockwell moved to Arlington, Virginia. Fire destroyed his studio in 1943, along with many of his drawings and paintings. Although he was saddened by the loss, Rockwell began painting more directly from life rather than relying on a model. Although he ceased working for *The Saturday Evening Post* in 1963, he continued to work for other magazines. He was associated with *Look* magazine from 1963–1973. He continued to paint pictures that depicted areas of deep concern to him—poverty, civil rights, and space exploration. He then spent the last years of his life traveling to foreign countries. Rockwell established a trust for his paintings and memorabilia to be displayed at the Norman Rockwell Museum in Stockbridge, Massachusetts. It houses the only major collection of Rockwell's work in the nation. Before Rockwell died in 1978, he was awarded the Presidential Medal of Freedom, the nation's highest civilian honor, for his "vivid and affectionate portraits of our country."

Art Appreciation *(cont.)*

Henri Matisse

One of the most important artists of the 20th century is Frenchman Henri Matisse. Born in 1869, he led an art movement called post-Impressionism and was one of the first famous collage artists. Throughout his productive and prolific career, Matisse's style continued to evolve as he experimented with different colors, art forms, and mediums. He did not follow the established rules of art; he created his own.

When Matisse was growing up, he did not have dreams of becoming a famous artist, but a twist of fate led him to that new career. While training to become a lawyer, he had to have surgery. During his recuperation his mother bought him some paints and a how-to book. From then on, Matisse was totally devoted to art. Matisse was encouraged in his artistic pursuits by his mother. She had exceptional artistic taste and talent of her own in creating decorative ceramics for the home. His father took a dim view of his son's new career path and, as Matisse was leaving for Paris, his father yelled out, "You'll starve!" However, his father did become supportive both financially and emotionally during hard times in the years that followed.

After one year at the Academie Julian, Matisse went on to study at the Academie Carriere. Throughout these early years he copied the Impressionistic style of painting and the Japanese style of woodblock prints. Oriental art, especially of Iran, with its strength of color and simplicity, stained glass windows from the Middle Ages, and European painting all impacted Matisse's style. As he came in contact with other styles, his work gradually changed.

In 1904 Matisse had his first one-man show, which met with little success. However, by the following year, he was the leader of the Fauvist movement, which relied on bright colors and distorted shapes. Critics were shocked by the new forms and called it the work of wild beasts, or Fauvism in French. While the actual movement lasted only a few years, its effects on the art world have been felt ever since.

Art Appreciation *(cont.)*

Henri Matisse *(cont.)*

In addition to painting, Matisse opened his own art academy for children in 1908. That same year, he published *Notes of a Painter,* in which he expressed his artistic beliefs. Later, he executed murals, created stage designs for a ballet, drew several series of book illustrations, and made sculptures and collages. (Collages are pictures made of different types of materials pasted together to give the artwork its design and texture.) The collage could be made entirely or partially of the different materials. They could include various papers, photographs, or cloths. Matisse's collages were some of the most important pieces of work that he ever produced. Even more impressive is the fact that he created many of them when he was in his eighties and sick in bed. He would instruct his assistants to paint huge pieces of paper with bright colors. Then he would cut out the shapes. As directed, the assistants pinned the shapes onto white paper and then pasted them down.

Matisse's style of painting brought harmony of space and color to his work. His paintings were simple but radiant and bright in color. They were not meant to be realistic, but rather focused on "form," not subject. The lines, colors, textures, and arrangement of objects in space were the focus of the painting in order to achieve the proper "form."

A man with a mischievous personality and keen sense of humor, Matisse brought these characteristics to his artwork. A master of color, he brought a special joyfulness and a childlike perspective to his art. When Matisse died in 1954, he left a part of himself behind for all future generations to enjoy.

Art Appreciation *(cont.)*

A. What procedure did Norman Rockwell follow when painting? Complete the chart below with the five main steps, in sequential order, that Rockwell followed in order to complete a painting.

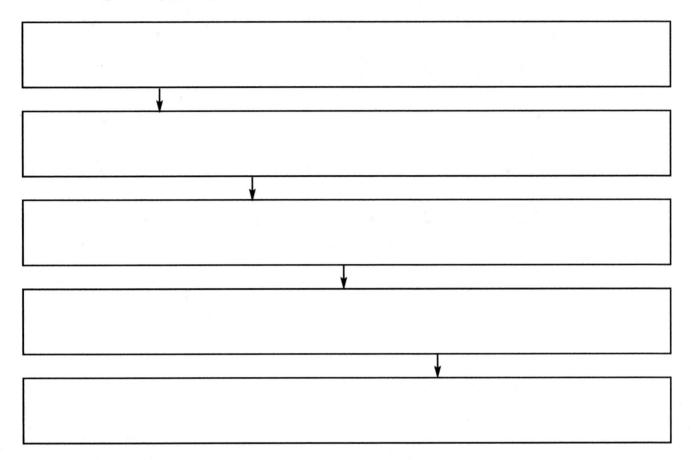

B. What path did Norman Rockwell pursue to achieve success and recognition as an American painter?

_____

_____

_____

_____

_____

_____

Art Appreciation *(cont.)*

C. How did Henri Matisse develop an interest in art?

_____

_____

_____

_____

_____

_____

_____

_____

Planning Section

Use the space below to plan your response to the essay question that appears on the following page. You may use a graphic organizer or web to help you plan your essay. Write your final essay on the lines provided below the essay question.

Art Appreciation (cont.)

Essay

Norman Rockwell and Henri Matisse are both famous artists of the twentieth century. How did their artwork impact the world of art and society? Use details from both reading selections.

In your response, be sure to include:

★ an explanation of how and what Rockwell painted

★ an explanation of the different stages of Matisse's career

★ which style of art you prefer and why

Check your essay for proper spelling, grammar, and punctuation.

_____

_____

_____

_____

_____

_____

_____

_____

_____

_____

_____

Open Arms

Directions: You are going to read a poem and a selection that deals with immigration into the United States from foreign nations.

First, you will complete a chart and two short-response questions. Then, you will write an essay about the two articles.

"The New Colossus"

"The New Colossus" is a poem written by a young Russian Jewish immigrant named Emma Lazarus. She wrote the poem to help raise funds for the pedestal for the Statue of Liberty. Emma Lazarus was not invited to the dedication ceremony in 1868, but her poem was finally recognized and attached to the base of the Statue of Liberty in 1903. Her poem has become world famous for focusing on the people coming to America, rather than the abstract concept of freedom.

The New Colossus

Not like the brazen giant of Greek fame,

With conquering limbs astride from land to land;

Here at our sea-washed, sunset gates shall stand

A mighty woman with a torch, whose flame

Is the imprisoned lightning, and her name

Mother of Exiles. From her beacon-hand

Glows world-wide welcome; her mild eyes command

The air-bridged harbor that twin cities frame.

"Keep, ancient lands, your storied pomp!" cries she

With silent lips. "Give me your tired, your poor,

Your huddled masses yearning to breathe free,

the wretched refuse of your teeming shore.

Send these, the homeless, tempest-tost, to me.

I lift my lamp beside the golden door!"

Open Arms

The Great Lady of the Harbor

Immigration has occurred since America was first discovered. From the earliest settlers to the present day, immigrants (people who come into a country from another country) have chosen the United States as a land of opportunity in which to prosper and be free.

Immigrants have many reasons for moving from country to country. Some of the major reasons for immigration are to find better jobs, to see a better way of life, and to escape persecution, war, starvation, and/or disease. Many of the new immigrants came by ship and sailed into New York Harbor, where they caught their first look at the Statue of Liberty.

The Statue of Liberty was a gift to the people of the United States from the people of France. Frederic Bartholdi designed and sculpted the statue. He was sent to America to complete his plans. As he sailed into the harbor at Bedloe's Island, he knew that was where the statue should be located. He decided to make the statue a lady, as a symbol of liberty. She would face the ocean, with a greeting and a promise to all who viewed her. He called the statue, "Liberty Enlightening the World." Barthodi talked to President Grant, and it was agreed that France would build the statue and the United States would build the base. It was given to the U.S. in 1884 and has since become a symbol of freedom to people all over the world. It was hoped that the statue would be ready in 1876 for the centennial celebration, but this was not possible due to France's involvement in a war with Prussia.

The statue is 151 feet and one inch (46.05 m) in height. It rests on top of a 154-foot (47 m) pedestal. The lady, holding a 21-foot (6.3-m) torch in her right hand, extends her 42-foot (12.6-m) arm upward. The highly visible and welcoming torch can be seen by all people of the world who enter or leave port. In her other arm, she cradles a tablet close to her body. The tablet is 13 feet seven inches (4.1 m) in width and 23 feet seven inches (7.1 m) in length. Upon her head rests a crown with seven spikes that reach out to the seven seas and the seven continents (North America, South America, Europe, Asia, Africa, Australia, and Antarctica). Each of the seven spikes stands for seven liberties: civil liberty, moral liberty, national liberty, natural liberty, personal liberty, political liberty, and religious liberty.

The Statue of Liberty, constructed of 100 tons of copper with a 125-ton steel frame, cost $250,000. It could not be set in place until enough funds were donated to build a pedestal on which it would rest. Many people visit the statue every year and climb the 171 steps to reach the torch. It is a national treasure.

Open Arms

A. Directions: First complete the chart and the two short response questions. Then answer the essay question. You may look back at the selections as often as necessary.

The Statue of Liberty

Seven Continents	Seven Liberties
1. _____	1. _____
2. _____	2. _____
3. _____	3. _____
4. _____	4. _____
5. _____	5. _____
6. _____	6. _____
7. _____	7. _____

B. Name three reasons immigrants came to America. Support your answer with examples of the liberties they were seeking to find.

_____

_____

_____

_____

_____

_____

_____

Open Arms

C. What type of new immigrant was being welcomed into the United States by the Statue of Liberty?

_____

_____

_____

_____

_____

_____

_____

Planning Section

Directions: Use the space below to plan your response to the essay question that appears on the following page. Write your final essay on the lines provided below the essay question.

Open Arms

Essay

Directions: Imagine that you are a poor young immigrant coming to America with your parents. Your boat is going to dock at the harbor in New York City. Write a letter to your grandparents who stayed in the country you left behind.

Be sure to include:

- ★ what you see greeting you in the harbor

- ★ how you feel seeing the Statue of Liberty for the first time

- ★ how you feel visiting the Statue of Liberty and reading Emma Lazarus's poem

Be sure to check your paper for spelling, grammar, and punctuation.

_____

_____

_____

_____

_____

_____

_____

_____

_____

_____

_____

_____

Being An Individual

Read "Flight" below and the article about Florence Nightingale on page 88. "Flight" describes the historic background of the Wright Brothers and the development of their aircraft. The article entitled "Florence Nightingale" tells of Florence Nightingale's heroic efforts to nurse soldiers during the Crimean War.

You will complete a chart and answer two short-response questions about the reading selections. Then you will write an essay about the two articles. You may look back at the articles as often as necessary.

Flight

At the turn of the century, very few believed that flight was possible in a heavier-than-air machine. Two of the few who did believe were Wilbur and Orville Wright. Wilbur Wright was born in 1867 in Indiana, and Orville was born four years later in Ohio. As children, the two were fascinated by mechanics and even earned small amounts of money by selling homemade mechanical toys. Both went to school, but neither received a high school diploma. When they grew up, Orville built a printing press and

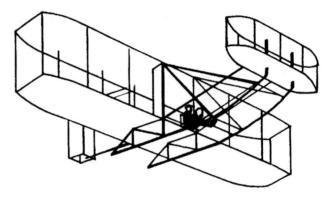

started a printing business, developing a weekly newspaper, which Wilbur edited. Next, they tried their hands at renting and selling bicycles, and finally they began to manufacture the bikes themselves.

In 1896, the brothers read about the death of a pioneer glider named Otto Lilienthal, and his work sparked their interest. They started to read everything available on aeronautics and soon became experts on the subject. The Wrights contacted the National Weather Bureau to determine the best place to carry out their flight experiments. The Bureau advised them to try a narrow strip of sandy land called Kill Devil Hill near Kitty Hawk, North Carolina. In 1900, they tested a glider that could hold a person, and in 1901 they tried again with a larger glider. Neither glider could lift as they had hoped, although they did achieve some success in controlling balance.

Being an Individual (cont.)

Flight (cont.)

The Wright Brothers felt confident that flight was possible. They theorized that previous information about air pressure on curved surfaces must be inaccurate. They built their own wind tunnel and over 200 model wings in order to make their own pressure tables. Their pressure tables became the first reliable ones ever made.

In 1902, they tried a third glider, using their new information. It vastly exceeded the success of all previous gliders, with some glides exceeding 600 feet (180 meters). This led the brothers to plan and build a power airplane. In 1903, at a cost just under one thousand dollars, the plane was complete. Its wings measured 40.5 feet (12 meters), and it weighed 750 pounds (340 kilograms) with the pilot. In September of 1903, they arrived in Kittyhawk, but a series of bad storms delayed them. However, on December 17, 1903, they achieved flight.

Over the next few years, their experiments produced even longer and better flights. On October 5, 1905, their plane flew for 24.2 miles (38.9 kilometers) in just over 38 minutes. In 1908, they closed a contract with the United States Department of War for the first military airplane ever made.

The brothers went on to exhibit flight in France and the United States, as well as to teach others to be pilots. Eventually, the inevitable happened. On September 17, 1908, Orville and his passenger, Lieutenant Thomas E. Selfridge, crashed due to a malfunction. Orville recovered, but Selfridge died. However, the work of the brothers continued until Wilbur died of typhoid fever in 1912. Orville carried on alone until his death in 1948. Today they are remembered as the fathers of modern flight.

Being an Individual *(cont.)*

Florence Nightingale

In 1854 a nurse named Florence Nightingale was determined to make a difference during the Crimean War. Nightingale organized a group of nurses to care for wounded British soldiers. She and the other nurses boarded a ship in England and set sail for a hospital in Scutari, Turkey. When they arrived at the hospital, the nurses saw that it was surrounded by mud and trash. However, the worst was yet to come. Upon entering the hospital, Nightingale and her nurses could not believe the deplorable conditions these soldiers had to endure. Everything in the hospital was dirty and falling apart. Rats moved about freely. Soldiers who were sick or injured lay on bed after bed. But there were not enough beds to go around, so many other soldiers were on the floor. The hospital had few supplies. The soldiers often went without food and medicine. Their was not enough clothing, blankets, or equipment.

The hospital's doctors and staff did not welcome the nurses. They felt the nurses would be more trouble than they were worth. They would not even allow the nurses to help the soldiers. The nurses were not given any supplies except for a daily pint of water intended for drinking and washing.

Every day, more sick and wounded soldiers arrived at the hospital from the battlefield. Conditions got increasingly worse, and the situation seemed hopeless. But Nightingale was more determined than ever to make the hospital a better place. Against army regulations, she went to Constantinople to purchase supplies. She made sure the orderlies cleaned and scrubbed everything in the hospital. She had the patients' clothes washed regularly. She managed to obtain money that was raised in England to buy additional supplies. Not only did Nightingale attend to all these administrative duties, she also spent countless hours caring for the sick and dying. The doctors were inspired by her dedication, and the soldiers felt that she was an angel of mercy. Nightingale ensured the survival of many soldiers who might otherwise have died.

In 1856, after the war ended, Nightingale went home to England. She was honored as a hero for her work in the Crimean War. Once home, Nightingale's commitment to helping others continued. She worked to improve the quality of army and civilian hospitals.

Being an Individual *(cont.)*

A. The Wright Brothers accomplished many things in their lifetimes. Using the information presented in "Flight," complete the chart by recording an accomplishment for each year listed below.

Year	Accomplishments
1900	
1901	
1902	
1903	
1905	
1908	

B. In what businesses were the Wright Brothers involved?

_____

_____

_____

_____

_____

_____

Being an Individual *(cont.)*

C. In the article "Florence Nightingale," what conditions did injured British soldiers face during the Crimean War? What things did Florence Nightingale do to make those conditions better?

_____

_____

_____

_____

_____

_____

_____

_____

_____

Planning Section

Use the space below to plan your response to the essay question that appears on the following page. You may use a graphic organizer or web to help you plan your essay. Write your final essay on the lines provided below the essay question.

Being an Individual *(cont.)*

Essay

Florence Nightingale and the Wright Brothers can be described as courageous, determined, adventuresome, confident, and individualistic. Choose two terms that describe these people. Use details from both selections to support your ideas.

In your response, be sure to include:

★ a topic sentence

★ the two terms and specific examples that demonstrate those characteristics

★ a concluding sentence

Check your essay for proper spelling, grammar, and punctuation.

_____

_____

_____

_____

_____

_____

_____

_____

_____

_____

_____

_____

Teeing Off

You are going to read two selections about famous golfers. One is about Nancy Lopez, and the other is about Lee Trevino.

First, you will fill in a visual organizer and answer two short-response questions. You will then write an essay using information from both selections. You may go back to the readings as often as necessary.

Nancy Lopez, Golfer

Nancy Lopez was born in Torrance, California, in 1957, while her parents were there visiting relatives. She actually grew up in Roswell, New Mexico, with her older sister, Delma, and her parents, Domingo and Marina.

In 1964, Marina, Nancy's mother, became ill with a lung disorder. The doctor recommended that she walk outside daily to strengthen her lungs. Marina thought that simply walking everyday would be boring, so she suggested that she and Domingo play golf together for her daily exercise. The only problem was what to do with Nancy. Nancy's sister was already married by that time and there was no one to babysit, so Nancy tagged along with her parents.

Little by little, Nancy would ask to participate in her parents' golf games. Her father taught her how to swing the club and hit the ball. When her father saw how interested she was in golf, he spent hours giving her golf lessons. When she asked for clubs of her own, her mother gladly gave hers to Nancy. When Nancy was nine years old, she won the state of New Mexico Pee Wee tournament, scoring well enough to win the junior competition. However, officials said that she was not old enough to compete with the juniors.

Teeing Off *(cont.)*

Nancy Lopez, Golfer *(cont.)*

By the age of 11, Nancy was invited to play in the New Mexico Women's Amateur Tournament. Nancy's father was very protective of her. He was concerned about her facing such competition at a young age, but she did well and was the runner up in the tournament. Her parents sacrificed and supported Nancy greatly. Her father was at her side, coaching her during practice, and her mother sewed her golf outfits. Her father even made a sand trap in the backyard because the local municipal golf course did not have one.

Nancy had her share of obstacles to overcome. The local country club would not sponsor her because she was Mexican American, and people often criticized her style. Lee Trevino, a famous Mexican-American golfer, encouraged her; and her parents worked hard to afford her the opportunity to go on tour. In 1977, she was named Women's Pro Rookie of the Year, and that was only the beginning of her success.

By 1995, she held 47 professional tournament championships and was a member of the LPGA (Ladies Professional Golf Association) Hall of Fame.

Teeing Off (cont.)

Lee Trevino, Golfer

Lee Trevino was born in Dallas, Texas, in 1939. He was raised by his mother, Juanita, who worked as a maid, and by his grandfather, Joe Trevino, who worked as a farmhand. When Lee was a little boy, he helped his grandfather pick cotton and work in the onion fields. Lee's grandfather took him hunting for rabbits to provide meat for the family's dinners. When Lee was seven years old, his grandfather got him a job as a gravedigger at a cemetery outside Dallas, where they moved into a small house with no running water, heat, or windows.

In this rural area, which years later became a suburb of Dallas, Lee noticed a green field where people were playing golf. He did not know what golf was at the time. Lee soon discovered that he could earn some money by finding lost golf balls and selling them back to the golfers. When he was eight years old, Lee became friends with the greenskeeper's son, and the two of them spent countless hours on the course when it was closed for business. The next job Lee got was as a caddie. His meager salary and his sometimes generous tips helped to sustain his family. He spent time with the caddies, playing and practicing. They shared an old set of clubs and bet each other for quarters. Lee Trevino never really had any formal golf instruction; he was primarily self-taught.

Teeing Off (cont.)

Lee Trevino, Golfer (cont.)

Lee left school at the age of 14 and was employed by Hardy Greenwood, who gave him a job at Hardy's Driving Range in Dallas. When Hardy's decided to expand and add a nine-hole course, Lee and another man designed and landscaped the whole 12 acres. At the age of 17, Lee Trevino joined the Marines. He continued to play golf as a Marine and was soon noticed by his superiors and reassigned to Special Services, where he played full-time golf. When he was discharged from the Marines, he went back to work for Greenwood. He continued practicing and playing tournaments. By 1965, Lee Trevino was ready to try the Professional Golf Association (PGA) tour, but it was not until two years later that he finally got the opportunity. In 1968, he won his first major professional tournament, the U.S. Open.

In 1970, he led the PGA in earnings and went on to win a second U.S. Open, as well as and the Canadian and British Opens the following year. He was named PGA Player of the Year and Sportsman of the Year in 1971. In 1975, Lee Trevino was struck by lightning while playing the Western Open. After several back surgeries and rehabilitation, Trevino was back on the golf course. He has had great success and passed the two-million-dollar mark in earnings in 1979. He was elected to the PGA and World Golf Halls of Fame in 1981. In 1990, he won seven of 26 Senior Tour events. He can be recognized by his sombrero logo and his nickname, "Supermex."

Teeing Off *(cont.)*

A. Compare the obstacles, training, and accomplishments of Nancy Lopez and Lee Trevino.

Nancy Lopez		Lee Trevino
	Problems/Obstacles	
	Training	
	Accomplishments	

B. Explain how Nancy Lopez's family encouraged her to pursue her interest in golf.

_____

_____

_____

_____

_____

_____

_____

_____

_____

_____

Teeing Off *(cont.)*

C. Why might Lee Trevino be considered a self-made man? Explain by using examples from the selection.

_____

_____

_____

_____

_____

_____

_____

_____

_____

Planning Section

Use the space below to plan your response to the essay question that appears on the following page. You may use a graphic organizer or web to help you plan your essay. Write your final essay on the lines provided below the essay question.

Teeing Off *(cont.)*

Essay

Nancy Lopez and Lee Trevino overcame obstacles they faced during their rise to fame as athletes. Explain why you do or do not feel that they would have been able to overcome these obstacles if they had not had the support of others.

In your response be sure to include:

★ an example of the support that each person had

★ examples from the selections of the obstacles each person faced

★ how their success was measured

Check your essay for correct grammar, punctuation, and spelling.

_____

_____

_____

_____

_____

_____

_____

_____

_____

_____

_____

On Ice

Read the article about figure skating and the biographical sketch entitled "Torvill and Dean." "Figure Skating" discusses the history of the sport and the different types of competitions. "Torvill and Dean" is about two world famous champion ice dancing partners.

First, you will complete a chart and two short response questions. Then you will write an essay about the two articles. You may look back at the articles as often as necessary.

Figure Skating

The earliest known reference to skating for pleasure was made in 1175 when people in London, England, "skated" on polished animal bones attached to their boots. They used sticks to push themselves along. The first skates with iron blades appeared in the Netherlands in the 1200s or 1300s. Because the iron blades were stronger than bone, skaters no longer needed sticks.

Originally, skaters performed rigid routines, tracing patterns on the ice. An American named Jackson Haines created a single-unit skate with the blade screwed into the sole. He was the first to add ballet, music, and colorful costumes to the sport. He toured Europe in 1864 to introduce his style of skating to the world. Skating became popular in North America, and the first covered rinks were built in the 1850s. Louis Rubinstein of Montreal, Canada, was the first great figure skater of North America. He won the Canadian championship for 12 years in a row, 1878–1889. Figure skating became an Olympic event in 1908.

Skating competitions have similar rules for the men's and women's divisions. The performers skate a technical program of two minutes and 40 seconds and a free-skating program of four minutes for women and four and one-half minutes long for men. In the technical program, there are eight required moves: three jumps, three spins, and two footwork moves. In the free-skate program, the skaters display their artistic and technical skills, with original choreography. Skaters are judged on technical merit and artistic impression for both programs. The free skate counts for two-thirds, and the technical program one-third, of the skater's total score.

Figure Skating *(cont.)*

Pairs skating began in Vienna, Austria, in the 1800s. The partners perform dangerous throws and lifts. The rules and scoring are similar to singles skating. The required elements include synchronized solo spins, side-by-side jumps, and overhead lifts and throws. Ice dancing is more musical and stylish than athletic. It became an Olympic sport in 1976. In ice dancing, the man is not allowed to lift the woman above his head. The competition has four parts: a two-minute original dance, a four-minute free dance, and two compulsory dances. The free dance is the most important, counting for 50 percent of the final score. In Canada there are two other popular forms of figure skating competitions—fours skating which is similar to pairs but with two men and two women; and precision skating for teams of 12 or more skaters.

Fifty countries belong to the International Skating Union (ISU), which supervises competitions at the junior world and world championships, European championships, and the Winter Olympics. Each country also has competitions at the national level. The United States Figure Skating Association sponsors competitions at eight different skill levels.

On Ice *(cont.)*

Torvill and Dean

Jayne Torvill and Christopher Dean were born in Nottingham, England. They are from middle class backgrounds—Jayne's parents owned a news agents' shop, and Chris's father was an electrician. Jane began skating at age nine, and Chris took up the sport after receiving skates for Christmas when he was 10 years old.

In 1971 Jayne Torvill won the British senior pairs championship with her partner, Michael Hutchinson. The next year Hutchinson moved to London and Torvill continued in solo skating competition. Christopher Dean began as an ice dancer with partner Sandra Elson. They were the British junior dance champions in 1974.

In 1975 Janet Sawbridge, a professional skater and mutual friend, suggested that Jayne and Chris try skating together. The pair enjoyed working together and made excellent progress. Janet was their coach and trainer.

By 1976 they were ready for European competitions in St. Gervais, France, and Obserstdorf, Germany. The pair entered the European and world championships in the winter of 1978. They began work with a new coach, Betty Callaway, following the world championships in Ottawa, Canada. She encouraged Torvill and Dean to polish their program and in 1978 they became the British ice skating champions. They continued to improve their standing in international tournaments. In 1980 Jayne Torvill and Chris Dean decided to leave their jobs to devote themselves to skating full time.

As a reward for commitment to their sport, Torvill and Dean placed first in all 1981 competitions, making them the British, European, and world champions in ice dancing. The pair began to develop their own choreography around a central theme for both short programs and free dance competitions. In 1984 their skating ability and creative choreography reached a high point with their free dance to Maurice Ravel's *Bolero*. They performed the dramatic love story at the 1984 Olympics in Sarajevo and became the only team in figure skating history to receive perfect 6.0 scores from all judges. Torvill and Dean returned to the Olympics 10 years later (1994) and won a bronze medal.

Jayne Torvill and Christopher Dean turned professional after the 1984 Olympics and toured the world with Ice Capades. Free from the restrictive rules of competitions, they have been able to bring their most innovative interpretations to ice dancing.

On Ice *(cont.)*

A. Compare and contrast Jayne Torvill and Christopher Dean by completing the Venn Diagram. Include ideas about their differences and similarities. Use details from the reading selection.

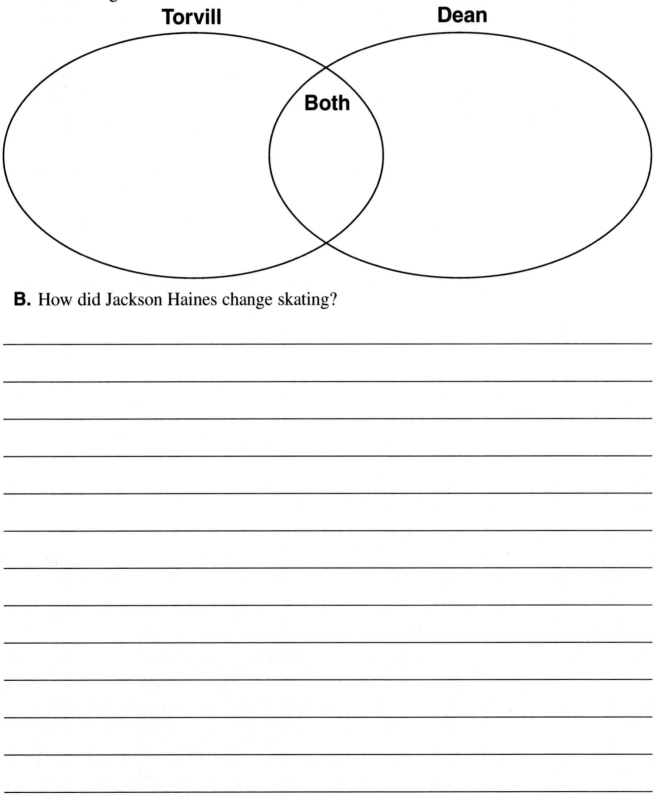

Torvill   **Dean**

Both

B. How did Jackson Haines change skating?

_____

_____

_____

_____

_____

_____

_____

_____

_____

_____

_____

_____

On Ice *(cont.)*

C. Identify three character traits that Torvill and Dean possess. Use specific details from the reading to support your response.

_____

_____

_____

_____

_____

_____

_____

_____

Planning Section

Use the space below to plan your response to the essay question that appears on the following page. You may use a graphic organizer or web to help you plan your essay. Write your final essay on the lines provided below the essay question.

On Ice *(cont.)*

Essay

Solo skating and paired skating are the two main categories of ice skating competitions. Compare and contrast the two types of skating. Explain how Torvill and Dean were successful partners. Use information from both reading selections.

In your response, be sure to include:

★ the requirements for each type of program—solo and paired

★ the success of Torvill and Dean

★ what a pair must consider to be successful in competition

★ what, besides good technical skating, makes a champion team

Check your essay for proper spelling, grammar, and punctuation.

_____

_____

_____

_____

_____

_____

_____

_____

_____

_____

_____

_____

Exploring Above and Below

Read the two articles about exploration of the unknown. "Underwater Exploration" explains the history of ocean exploration. "Space: The Quest for the Final Frontier" discusses some aspects of the space program.

You will complete a chart and answer two short-response questions about the reading selections. Then you will write an essay about the two articles. You may look back at the articles as often as necessary.

Underwater Exploration

Explorers not only venture to new and unknown lands, but also into the seas. Without sophisticated technology to explore in deep water, the oceans once held many more mysteries than they do now. Not until the 1930s and 1940s did underwater explorers begin to gather information about the world beneath the sea.

In 1934, William Beebe invented an undersea exploratory device called a bathysphere. The bathysphere was a round craft in which the diver was lowered into the ocean by a wire rope. A major flaw of the bathysphere, however, was its weight. If the rope securing it to the ship broke, it would sink to the ocean floor. There would be no escape for the unfortunate diver trapped in a fallen bathysphere.

Professor Auguste Piccard refined the design of the bathysphere and called his invention a bathyscaphe. The bathyscaphe was suspended from a large buoyancy tank that had the ability to keep the device afloat. In addition, the bathyscaphe contained a ballast filled with iron pellets that, when released by the diver, could allow the craft to come to the surface. This safety feature decreased the diver's danger while exploring the undersea world.

Exploring Above and Below *(cont.)*

Underwater Exploration *(cont.)*

Science and technology combined to create modern diving equipment. Early divers carried cylinders of oxygen on their backs and breathed the gas through a mouthpiece connected to the tank with a hose. The tank supplied only two hours worth of oxygen and only highly skilled divers were able to use the awkward breathing apparatus. Another unfortunate drawback that was discovered was that oxygen used below a certain depth becomes a poisonous gas—carbon monoxide.

In the 1940s, Jacques-Yves Cousteau and Emile Gagnan found a solution to this problem. They invented the aqualung, or SCUBA gear. The aqualung was filled with a mixture of gases resembling Earth's atmosphere, rather than pure oxygen. The gear also provided the diver with this gas mixture at a pressure appropriate for swimming deep below the ocean's surface.

Jacques-Yves Cousteau

In addition, deep-sea diving suits have been invented that allow divers to go as deep as 2000 feet (600 meters). These suits resemble space suits and give the divers the flexibility to get close to the organisms they are observing. Recently, large underwater vehicles have been invented which allow divers to remain at the ocean bottom for over two weeks. These scientific advancements have made underwater exploration safer for courageous men and women, as well as improving their abilities to study the organisms and the ocean waters. These explorations have revealed new knowledge about plant and animal life, including alternative energy and food sources to help humankind.

Exploring Above and Below *(cont.)*

Space: The Quest for the Final Frontier

"Seventy-five feet . . . things looking good . . . lights on . . . kicking up some dust. Thirty feet . . . contact light . . . engine stop," said Edward "Buzz" Aldrin as he and Neil Armstrong approached the moon's surface.

"Houston. Tranquility Base here. . . . The *Eagle* has landed," Armstrong added as the pair became the first men in history to reach the moon on July 20, 1969, at 4:17 P.M. Eastern Standard Time. The National Aeronautics and Space Administration (NASA), however, had been preparing for this momentous event for a long time. Journey back into the history of space exploration and look at a few of these courageous modern-day adventurers whose work made NASA's visions a reality.

The first man to make any sort of journey into space (and later, to orbit the planet) was Soviet Major Yuri Gagarin. The first American citizen to explore this frontier was Navy Lieutenant commander Alan Shepard. Shepard's flight was considered to be a success as the rocket in which he rode, *Mercury-Redstone 2*, blasted 116 miles above the earth.

As humankind pushed into the vastness of space, a notable mission piloted by Colonel John Glenn was launched. NASA's goal was for Glenn to fly the spacecraft, *Friendship 7*, in three orbits around the Earth. Within five hours, Glenn witnessed the sun rise and set three times. When his mission was complete, Glenn began his dangerous descent into Earth's atmosphere, but the heat shield on the spacecraft loosened.

The heat shield was located on the bottom of the space capsule. Its function was to protect Glenn from the extreme heat encountered upon reentry into the atmosphere. If the heat shield had separated from the capsule, Glenn would have burned to death. Fortunately, the heat shield stayed in place, and the capsule carrying Glenn landed safely in the ocean. The courage of these early space navigators was demonstrated once again.

Space . . . *(cont.)*

As the years passed, NASA commissioned a series of space flights known as Project Gemini, which involved spacecrafts built for two. Each of these missions contributed to our knowledge of space, but one outstanding achievement of this mission occurred when astronaut Edward White walked in space for the first time with only a 24-foot line connecting him to his spacecraft.

Unfortunately, Edward White and fellow astronauts Gus Grissom and Roger Chafee met with disaster when they died in an accident while training for the first Apollo flight. In a speech made before Congress, John Glenn spoke of the great dangers associated with space exploration with these words: "Not every flight can come back as successfully as the three we have had so far. There will be failures. There will be sacrifices." The Apollo program did continue, culminating in *Apollo 11,* which landed on the moon in 1969. As Neil Armstrong stepped onto the lunar surface, he uttered the famous words, "This is one small step for man, one giant leap for mankind."

The NASA space program has continued to conduct scientific probes into outer space. It has launched probes like the Pioneer and Voyager spacecraft to explore the moon, the planets, and other parts of the solar system. The Hubble Space Telescope and communications satellites like Echo and Telstar relay information back to Earth about our final frontier. Space stations circle our planet. What the future holds for humankind is in the minds and imaginations of our scientists! The possibilities for the future are endless!

Exploring Above and Below *(cont.)*

A. What are five major achievements in the world of underwater exploration? Complete the chart in the order in which the events occurred.

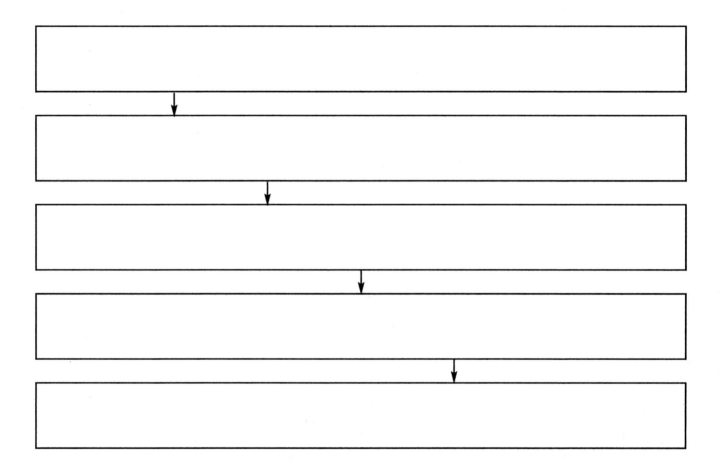

B. What problem existed with the original modern diving equipment?

_____

_____

_____

_____

_____

_____

_____

Exploring Above and Below *(cont.)*

C. What major problem did John Glenn have to worry about when he was ready to return into Earth's atmosphere after flying *Friendship 7* around Earth three times?

_____

_____

_____

_____

_____

_____

_____

_____

_____

Planning Section

Use the space below to plan your response to the essay question that appears on the following page. You may use a graphic organizer or web to help you plan your essay. Write your final essay on the lines provided below the essay question.

Exploring Above and Below *(cont.)*

Essay

Underwater exploration and exploration of outer space are alike in many ways. What are some ways in which exploring these two very different environments are similar? Use details from both reading selections.

In your response, be sure to include:

★ personality/character traits of the astronauts and aquanauts (divers)

★ equipment used

★ problems that could be encountered

Check your essay for proper spelling, grammar, and punctuation.

_____

Technological Advancements

Read the articles entitled "The Technological Home and Office" and "The TV Generation." The articles discuss computers, VCRs, and television. These electronic devices, invented during the twentieth century, have changed society.

You will complete a chart and answer two short response questions after reading the selections. Then you will write an essay about the two articles. You may look back at the articles as often as needed.

The Technological Home and Office

The average American home of the '80s differed quite a bit from the same home in the '70s, and technology was the reason. Suddenly it seemed there were new technologies to handle a variety of tasks. Answering machines took phone messages, video-cassette recorders (VCRs) taped television shows when people were not home to watch them, cable television broadened the spectrum of television viewing options, compact discs (CDs) enhanced sound of recorded music, and personal computers rapidly became exciting new sources of entertainment and productivity. Perhaps most significant and influential in the technologic advances of the decade of the '70s were the VCR and the personal computer.

VCRs

VCRs brought about a revolution in the entertainment industry. Previously, the choice of films was limited to what could be seen in theaters or the occasional few that were screened on network television. Children of the middle decades of the century can recall special television events when popular movies such as *The Wizard of Oz* were broadcast annually. With the advent of VCRs, people could buy or rent video tapes of movies and watch them whenever they chose. They could also record any movie or show from television to watch at their leisure. Some even began watching a show on one channel while taping one on another. With the dawn of the VCR came a new line of stores that sold and rented videos. This became one of the fastest growing industries of the 1980s.

Initially developed in the late '50s and early '60s, VCR technology grew from the need of television studios for a reliable method of recording programs for viewing in different time zones or for repeat usage. These early systems were far too complex and expensive for home use, however. In 1975 Sony Corporation introduced its Betamax, based on the system used by stations and networks. Matsushita Electric Industrial Corporation quickly released a competing system called Video Home System, or VHS. When the VHS system was adopted by the leading American television manufacturer, popularity of the Betamax waned. The VCR industry boomed throughout the '80s.

Technological Advancements *(cont.)*

The Technological Home and Office *(cont.)*

PCs

The personal computer also took off in popularity during the decade. In 1979 only 325,000 Americans had personal computers in their homes, but by 1984 the number of owners had climbed to 15 million.

The first home computers were used primarily for entertainment, with such games as Space Invaders and Pac Man. Advances in microchip technology and the availability of affordable equipment, such as modems and user-friendly software, led to growing awareness of the computer's usefulness, particularly to students. By 1985, students had become the largest users of personal computers.

While the price of both VCRs and personal computers has dropped over time, VCRs are usually more affordable for the average family, while personal computers are still relatively expensive. However, most schools have computers so that students are exposed to them before entering into the business world, where they are a staple.

The TV Generation

Children born in the late 1940s were the first generation to grow up with television. The full impact of this phenomenon would not be seen for many years.

History

During the late 1940s some television programs debuted, but they reached relatively small audiences. In 1948, there were fewer than 17,000 TV sets in the whole United States. By the end of the 1950s Americans owned an estimated 50 million sets.

Criticism

Criticism of the new industry came quickly. Some called the TV an "idiot box" or the "boob tube," claiming that many programs had little value. Educators were concerned about the impact of TV on their students and worried that students might skip their homework to watch shows. The amount of violence and sex depicted in some programs was also worrisome to many.

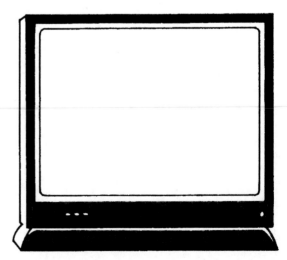

Technological Advancements *(cont.)*

The TV Generation *(cont.)*

Lifestyle Changes

Almost overnight the lifestyles of millions of Americans changed, as people stayed up later to watch shows. Some people stayed inside their homes more. With the invention of the TV dinner in 1954, some families even began eating in front of the television set.

Impact

One important impact of television was the business of TV commercials, which brought in over 1.5 billion dollars in advertising money in the early 1950s. Another way television impacted America was the coast-to-coast programs which allowed people to view firsthand historical events, such as political conventions and presidential inaugurations.

A Scandal

Quiz shows were popular during the '50s, but *Twenty-One* created the scandal of the decade. Players answered questions, and if they were correct, they could choose to keep going. As the questions grew more and more difficult, the prize money grew larger. One contestant, college instructor Charles Van Doren, amassed $129,000 in prize money. In 1958, however, a Congressional investigation revealed that the show was fraudulent and had given questions to Van Doren and others in advance.

TV Today

In the years since its invention, television has taken on a new look. With the advent of cable television and satellite dishes, hundreds of programs are readily available with a "click" of the remote control. Audiences are able to view hundreds of movies, sporting events, musical events, and a wide variety of programming at any given time. Endless possibilities exist for television programming in the future.

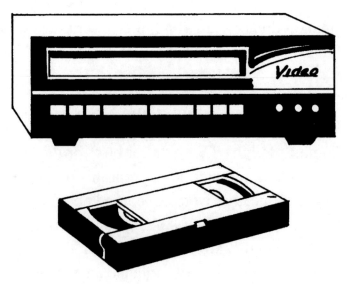

Technological Advancements *(cont.)*

A. Complete the chart by identifying the name of the invention, its abbreviated form, and its contribution to society.

Invention	Abbreviation	Contribution

B. How did VCRs change the entertainment industry? Use details from the selection and your own experience to answer the question.

_____

_____

_____

_____

_____

_____

_____

_____

_____

Technological Advancements *(cont.)*

C. Which problems facing television viewers today are the same as the problems that existed for the television viewers in the 1950s?

_____

_____

_____

_____

_____

_____

_____

_____

_____

Planning Section

Use the space below to plan your response to the essay question that appears on the following page. You may use a graphic organizer or web to help you plan your essay. Write your final essay on the lines provided below the essay question.

Technological Advancements *(cont.)*

Essay

Write an essay comparing VCRs, personal computers, and televisions. Use ideas from both reading selections.

In your response, be sure to include:

★ how these electronic devices are alike

★ how these electronic devices are different

★ how problems of censorship exist with each of these electronic devices

Check your essay for proper spelling, grammar, and punctuation.

_____

_____

_____

_____

_____

_____

_____

_____

_____

_____

_____

_____

_____

Earth's Natural Biomes

Read the articles entitled "Water Biomes" and "Land Biomes." Biomes are large bodies of water or land with similar climatic conditions, such as precipitation, sunlight, humidity, and/or temperature. The water article discusses freshwater and saltwater biomes. The land article summarizes the environmental conditions and the types of plant and animal organisms that inhabit the six major life zones.

You will complete a chart and answer two short-response questions after reading the selections. Then you will write an essay about the two articles. You may look back at the articles as often as necessary.

Water Biomes

A biome refers to a geographic location or life zone on the earth's land or water that is characterized by climatic environmental conditions, such as amount of precipitation, sunlight, humidity, and/or temperature. The specific climate of a biome determines the kinds of plants or animals that can survive there. Biomes of the land include coniferous, deciduous, and tropical forests, as well as deserts, tundras, and grasslands. Water biomes are classified as freshwater or marine. Currents, water pressure, and salinity contribute significantly to the organisms that can survive in a given water biome.

Freshwater

Freshwater ecosystems are contained in streams and rivers (running-water sources) and lakes and ponds (still-water sources). Water turbidity, dissolved oxygen, suspended particles, temperature, and currents contribute to the survival of particular species. Flowing water sources contain more dissolved oxygen due to greater mixing with air. However, running water  leaves large areas lacking the nutrients required for plankton to survive. Algae and freshwater plants anchor to rocks and pebbles as an adaptation to the water currents.

Earth's Natural Biomes *(cont.)*

Water Biomes *(cont.)*

Insect larvae inhabit this location by grasping plants with their hooks or suckers. Where freshwater flow is slow, many plants occupy river or stream banks. Snails, crayfish, and bass are some of the organisms making up the living communities existing there. In lakes and ponds where freshwater is very still, rooted plants are common. Plankton and algae are bountiful, often blocking sunlight to lower depths. Worms, bacteria, and fungi exist in deep, dark regions near the water's bottom. Insects (for example, dragonflies, mosquitoes, and gnats), frogs, fish, birds, and snakes inhabit shores of freshwater biomes.

Marine

Oceans, which make up 70% of the earth's surface, contain the greatest variety of species and are considered the largest biome of the earth. Light, temperature, salinity level, and water pressure are determining factors as to what organisms will occupy which regions of a marine environment. Light sources dwindle, temperatures decrease, and greater water pressure occurs with increasing depths. Marine biomes are divided into zones characterized by conditions that dictate the forms of life occupying a region. Coasts are located in the littoral zone (areas affected by tides, interfacing with beaches). This shallow zone includes tide-pool organisms (for example, starfish, kelp, and crabs) adaptable to wet and dry conditions. These organisms cling to rocks or burrow in sand.

The sublittoral zone extends beyond the continental shelf and is populated by protozoa and algae due to rich nutrients and ideal sunlight exposure. The pelagic zone comprises the deeper, darker marine regions. Food is scarce, and conditions are governed by water pressure and lack of light. Bacteria thrive on seafloors. Food chains consist of small fish, predatory fish, sharks, and rays. Also, marine mammals (whales and dolphins) inhabit marine biomes.

Earth's Natural Biomes *(cont.)*

Land Biomes

There are six major types of land biomes that dominate the earth.

Taiga or Coniferous Forest

Cone-bearing trees and shrubs that thrive in cold winters are found in this biome. These trees do not loose their leaves during the winter months; they remain green all year long. Bears, elk, deer, moose, lynx, porcupine, squirrels, and many varieties of insect inhabit coniferous forest. Conifers make up about 30% of the world's forests.

Deciduous Forest

Moderate temperature and precipitation are characteristic of this biome. A variety of broad-leaved trees that lose their leaves annually—such as maple, oak, and beech—form the canopy, the uppermost layer of the forest. The understory (a lower layer of trees) is made by birch, aspen, and pine trees, where many insects and birds dwell. The lower levels are formed by shrub-like vegetation, providing food for raccoons, opossum, mice, deer, snakes, and insects. Fallen branches and dead leaves are home to many animals.

Desert

Prolonged periods of extreme dryness and heat are typical here. Temperatures often exceed 100 degrees F (35° C) during daylight; however, they can drop quickly at night. Xerophitic (drought-tolerant) plants, such as cacti and succulents, have adapted to such extreme conditions because of their widespread root systems, tapping into the ground water. Owls, vultures, and hawks are some of the predators/scavengers here. Reptiles thrive and tarantulas and scorpions are common. Foxes, rabbits, bats, camels, and mice have learned to adapt to the desert's harshness by requiring less water for survival and by being nocturnal, hunting at night.

Grassland

This biome is characterized by large, open areas of land covered by rich, plush grasses. Typically, summers are warm and winters are cool. Grasslands are located on six of the seven continents of the world. They are too moist to become deserts and not rich enough to be forests. Dry winds and brush fires are common in this biome. Zebras, prairie dogs, mice, coyotes, and kangaroos occupy grasslands. Many mammals graze these areas for survival.

Earth's Natural Biomes *(cont.)*

Land Biomes *(cont.)*

Rain Forest

Wet, warm, and humid conditions are the norm of this biome. Broad-leaved evergreens, ferns, and orchids are deciduous and make up the forest's layers. The canopy level is usually so dense that little sunlight penetrates to the lower levels, so the floor is covered by fungi and mosses rather than by shrubbery. Many exotic birds and monkeys live in the canopies. At lower levels, insects are abundant. Various species of snakes, lizards, and other reptiles are common; and eagles, jaguars, and leopards are predators of small game.

Tundra

Mostly cold and dry conditions characterize this biome. Days are long in summer; in winter, brief daylight is typical. Plants with short spreading roots grow close to the ground, where temperatures are warmest and protection from the frigid winds is greatest. The plants include mosses, lichen, and short-flowering plants, adapted to life in areas covered by snow most of the year. No trees grow in the tundra due to the permafrost, ground that is permanently frozen. Only the top layer of the ground defrosts during the few warm summer months. Many birds, such as geese, ducks, and gulls, nest in the low-lying vegetation. In the summer, the snow melts slightly, leaving a soggy ground. As winter approaches, the birds migrate south. Caribou, polar bears, hares, foxes, wolves, and owls are inhabitants of tundra regions. These animals have adapted to the harsh conditions by producing warm furs and camouflaging, or blending in, with their surroundings.

Earth's Natural Biomes *(cont.)*

A. Examine the ways freshwater and marine biomes are alike and different. Determine which organisms exist only in freshwater biomes, which exist only in marine biomes, and which exist in both water biomes. List the organisms in the appropriate sections of the diagram below.

Freshwater	Both	Marine (Saltwater)

B. What are the two types of freshwater biomes, and how do they differ?

_____

_____

_____

_____

_____

_____

_____

_____

_____

Earth's Natural Biomes *(cont.)*

C. Why do only small shrubs, mosses, and short flowering plants grow in the tundra and not any type of trees?

_____

_____

_____

_____

_____

_____

_____

_____

_____

Planning Section

Use the space below to plan your response to the essay question that appears on the following page. You may use a graphic organizer or web to help you plan your essay. Write your final essay on the lines provided below the essay question.

Earth's Natural Biomes *(cont.)*

Essay

Many different environmental conditions affect the types of organisms that inhabit a particular life zone or biome. What are the conditions that exist in three or four of the biomes that determine the plant and animal life that live there? Use information from both readings.

In your response, be sure to include:

★ an introduction explaining what a biome is

★ the name of each biome and its environmental conditions

★ examples of plant and animal life in each

★ adaptations necessary in order for the organism to survive

Check your essay for proper spelling, grammar, and punctuation.

_____

_____

_____

_____

_____

_____

_____

_____

_____

_____

_____

_____

Plants

You are going to read two selections about plants. The first one, "Plants –Simple or Complex?" will discuss how plants are grouped. The second, "Growing Up," will be about the development of a plant seed.

First you will complete a chart and two short-response questions. Then you will write an essay about the two articles. You may look back at the articles as often as necessary.

Plants—Simple or Complex?

Plants can be divided into two groups, simple plants and complex plants.

Simple plants are found everywhere in nature. Algae are examples of simple plants that have the ability to live in freshwater, saltwater, soil, and on animals. Algae can make their own food. Their cells contain chloroplasts, a structure that holds a green substance called chlorophyll. Chlorophyll is the chemical substance needed by a plant to perform photosynthesis. During photosynthesis, the plant uses water, carbon dioxide, minerals, and the sun's energy to produce its own food.

Not all simple plants are capable of making their own food. Fungus is an example of a plant that must live off a host or another plant or animal for its food. Some common fungi are yeast and mushrooms. Most bacteria also need a food source, or host, off which to live. Mold, a common type of bacteria, is in this category.

Simple plants are also non-vascular. This means that simple plants do not have tubes called xylem and phloem. Xylem carries water and minerals up through the stem to the leaves, while the phloem carries the dissolved food down from the leaves, where it was made, to other parts of the plant. Most simple plants grow close to the ground as a result of their structure.

Plants *(cont.)*

Plants—Simple or Complex? *(cont.)*

Another characteristic of simple plants is that they grow in clumps or mats. Simple plants grow to maturity very quickly but do not produce embryos (small developing plants).

Most complex plants are found on land. Complex plants are vascular in structure. They have bundles of xylem and phloem that bring water and nutrients up the stems and into the leaves and flowers of the plant. Vascular plants produce their own food by performing photosynthesis, usually in their green leaves.

Remember, it is the green coloring of the chlorophyll in the chloroplasts that indicates photosynthesis. Complex plants reproduce themselves by producing embryos. They have true root systems, stems, and leaves. Unlike the simple plants, the complex plants can grow tall and wide and are easily recognizable. Deciduous trees, conifers, ferns, and flowering plants are all types of complex plants.

Plants *(cont.)*

Growing Up

Imagine you are a tiny, tiny seed inside a seed packet with hundreds of other seeds. It is very dark inside the packet—you can't see anything. You feel very, very crowded with all the other seeds in there pushing up against you, squeezing you between them. Suddenly, you hear a loud tearing noise—RIP!—and light flashes in your eyes. It is the sun.

But look out! Two big fingers are reaching into your seed packet, and they are coming straight at you! Pinch! They got you! The fingers pull you up, up, and out of the seed packet, into the sunlight. Then all of a sudden they let you go. Down, down, down you drop—into a hole in the earth. A giant hand pushes soil on top of you. Now it is dark again.

It is cool in the earth, and your body can feel and smell the dampness of the ground.

Time passes. You feel a need to stretch. First your seed coat cracks open and you send out a tiny, hair-like root down deep into the wet, cool soil to find the minerals and water you need to live and grow.

Time passes. Now you start to feel warmer, warmer, warmer. You feel a need to stretch again. This time you stretch upward as you grow. Up, up you grow with your stem moving toward the surface of the earth. You are defying the downward force of gravity! You break through!

Ah! You feel the warmth on your face. It feels good. You breathe deeply now and stretch out even more. Your leaves slowly grow out, uncurling to catch even more of the sun's light. You feel yourself growing stronger with the sun's touch. The sun is giving you the power you need to mix together the things you need to make food—your chlorophyll, the water and minerals from the soil, and the carbon dioxide from the air. This new food will help you grow stronger and stronger.

It is quiet now. You have made a beautiful flower. You know that this flower will make the seeds necessary to produce your next generation. Others like you will live on. Feel yourself rock gently back and forth as the wind pushes softly against your stem and leaves. Feel your roots stretching deeper into the soft, moist soil, helping you to stand tall in the wind. You feel warm, comfortable, and very content.

Plants *(cont.)*

A. Directions: Complete the chart by listing the distinguishing characteristics of simple and complex plants.

	Simple Plants	Complex Plants
Location		
Structure		
Characteristics		
Examples		

B. Compare the distinguishing characteristics of a simple plant to those of a complex plant.

_____

_____

_____

_____

_____

_____

_____

_____

Plants *(cont.)*

C. Identify three elements necessary for the successful growth of the plant. Use specific details from the reading to support your response.

Planning Section

Use the space below to plan your response to the essay question that appears on the following page. You may use a graphic organizer or web to help you plan your essay. Write your final essay on the lines provided below the essay question.

Plants *(cont.)*

Essay

Authors must decide why they are writing a particular passage. Their purpose may be to teach the reader something about a new topic, to persuade or convince the reader to think a certain way or support a view, or the author may simply wish to amuse the reader. Explain the intention of the writers of both selections. Use examples to support your answer.

In your response, be sure to include:

★ how the language was used to accomplish the author's purpose

★ how the mood was used to accomplish the author's purpose

★ why one selection might be more effective than another

Check your essay for proper spelling, grammar, and punctuation.

_____

_____

_____

_____

_____

_____

_____

_____

_____

_____

_____

_____

Splitting Genes

Read the articles entitled "Gregor Mendel" and "Barbara McClintock." Both articles are biographies of famous scientists in the field of genetics.

First you will complete the chart and answer two short response questions. Then you will write an essay about the two articles. You may look back at the articles as often as necessary.

Gregor Mendel

It is hard to imagine that an Augustinian monk (a member of a religious order) of the nineteenth century would provide the basis for modern genetics. However, that is precisely what happened.

Born in 1822 in Heinzendorf (near Austria), Gregor Mendel learned his love of gardening from his father who was a farmer.

Gregor attended high school in a nearby town. Since his family was poor and could not afford to pay the full tuition, Gregor received only half the amount of food as the other boys. He nearly starved, and the experience remained in his memory forever. On the advice of a professor he greatly admired, Gregor entered the monastery, where he could continue his studies. There he became the caretaker of the gardens and a substitute teacher in an elementary school.

From 1856 until 1864, Mendel worked with 10,000 specimen pea plants. He cross-fertilized 22 kinds of peas and studied seven characteristics of the plants. After eight years of accurate record-keeping, he formulated three laws that became the basis of the science of heredity. Gregor expounded the theory that some genes were dominant genes and other genes were recessive. The dominant genes were the stronger genes and masked the appearance of the recessive, or weaker, genes. He explained that genes were found in pairs: one gene was contributed by each parent. As a result, the characteristics that the new plant or offspring had was the result of the combination of the parent genes.

Splitting Genes *(cont.)*

Gregor Mendel *(cont.)*

When Mendel used pea plants, he crossed tall pea plants with short pea plants. The result was a hybrid plant, or one that showed the trait of being tall but carried the recessive gene of shortness. When hybrid pea plants were crossed, they produced both dominant and recessive pea plants.

He proudly wrote a paper to describe his findings. No one seemed to recognize the genius of his work, though, and Gregor was crushed. In 1883, he died of a heart attack. At that time, he was still embittered that no one recognized or appreciated his scientific revelations.

In 1990, three botanists from three different countries completed papers on the heredity of plants. Each of them had come across Mendel's paper when they made a routine check of the scientific literature before they published their own findings.

In each case, Mendel's forgotten paper reached the same conclusions that they had reached. Gregor Mendel's time had finally come.

Splitting Genes *(cont.)*

Barbara McClintock

No one would listen to Barbara McClintock's theory when she read her research paper describing her six years of lab work. In the late 1960s, fellow scientists at the Carnegie Institute of Washington in Cold Spring Harbor, New York, heard McClintock state that heredity was not fixed by parents of a child. They ignored her. She worked alone year after year, studying corn and its chromosome structures, which are responsible for inherited characteristics.

Barbara was born on June 16, 1902, in Hartford Connecticut. She was considered a tomboy in her youth. She asked for a set of tools when she was six years old and was the only girl on her neighborhood baseball team. Her parents objected to her going to college because they were afraid no man would want to marry her. She attended Cornell University in Ithaca, New York, where she majored in botany. While working toward her doctorate, she turned to plant genetics. This interest in the inherited traits in plants led to discoveries and theories that would have an impact in the field of genetics.

Barbara conducted her experiments on pairs of corn chromosomes. Barbara noticed in her work that there seemed to be elements that controlled a chromosome. She wanted to discover the effect x-rays would have on the genetic makeup of the corn. She discovered that the coloring of corn, usually bright yellow, speckled, or pale could be altered. Genes could change. She discovered that the coloring of corn and the spots were due to dynamic and mobile elements within the cell. She found that genes could "jump," or indulge in random behavior and could even pass from cell to cell. She even suggested that chromosomes changed only when attacked by a virus from the outside.

McClintock's work is significant because of its impact on Down's Syndrome. She was also involved in the study of antibiotic-resistant bacteria, a cure for African Sleeping Sickness, and the affects of cancer within the body. She opened the door to a future where people may be able to choose the genetic makeup of their children or cure diseases before the children are born.

She was granted an honorary doctorate from Harvard University in 1979 and won the first McArthur Laureate Award.

For over 50 years, McClintock worked tirelessly, without the help of lab assistants, in her maize patch. She was content with her quiet lifestyle and died peacefully in 1992. Some have said that her genius was not recognized by other scientists because she was so far ahead of her time. One hundred years from now people may understand all the implications of her work.

Splitting Genes *(cont.)*

A. Note the obstacles, areas of study, and awards Barbara McClintock faced during her life.

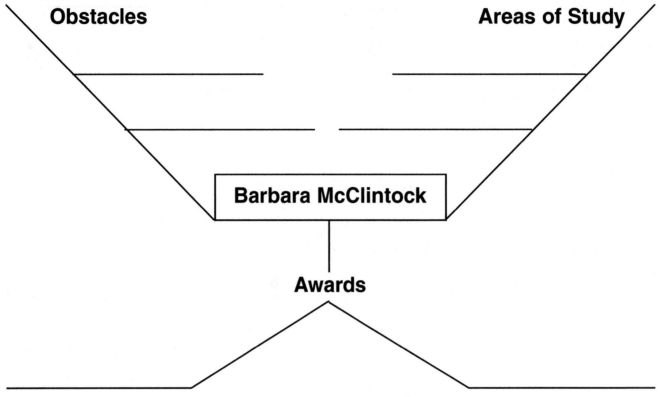

Obstacles

Areas of Study

Barbara McClintock

Awards

B. How did Gregor Mendel's work help people understand the science of inherited characteristics?

_____

_____

_____

_____

_____

_____

_____

_____

_____

_____

Splitting Genes *(cont.)*

C. According to Gregor Mendel's theory, what is the difference between a dominant and a recessive gene?

_____

_____

_____

_____

_____

_____

_____

_____

_____

Planning Section

Use the space below to plan your response to the essay question that appears on the following page. You may use a graphic organizer or web to help you plan your essay. Write your final essay on the lines provided below the essay question.

Splitting Genes *(cont.)*

Essay

Both Gregor Mendel and Barbara McClintock were scientists who laid the foundation for the study of genetics today. In your essay, explain why this is true. Use details from both selections.

In your response, be sure to include:

★ the theories stated by Gregor Mendel and Barbara McClintock

★ the contribution each scientist made to the study of genetics

★ why each scientist could be considered the founder of genetics

Check your essay for correct grammar, punctuation and spelling.

_____

_____

_____

_____

_____

_____

_____

_____

_____

_____

_____

Electrifying Forces

You are going to read two articles about electricity. The article "Electricity" will tell you about voltage, current, and amps. The article about electric meters will tell about how electric companies find out how much electricity is being used in your home.

First, you will complete a chart and two short response questions. Then you will write an essay about the two articles. You may look back at the articles as often as necessary.

Electricity

Electricity is the movement of electrons. Electrons are negatively charged particles. They are attracted to positively charged particles called protons.

When an electron moves, trying to reach a proton, an electrical force is created. This pushing power, or force, is called the voltage. The harder the electrons push, the greater the force created. This greater force means a higher voltage exists. If there are few electrons pushing, a weak force exists and there is low voltage. Voltage is measured in units called volts.

Current is the actual movement of electrons. The more electrons that are actually moving from a negative region to the positive region, the greater the current. The current does not tell the speed at which the electrons are moving, just the number of electrons that move. Current is measured in a unit called amperes (amps).

The current in a circuit can be controlled or regulated. Resistors are devices that can change the number of electrons that flow through the circuit. Resistors are often used in light-dimmer switches. When a switch is left fully open, electrons can flow through the wires of the circuit easily. The electrons will flow to the light bulb and the bulb will glow brightly. This is a circuit with low resistance. As the switch is regulated, or dimmed, fewer electrons flow through the circuit. The resistor is allowing less current to flow to the light bulb, and the result is that the light is dimmer. This is a circuit with high resistance.

The amp is proportional to the number of electrons moving past a point in a wire each second. This is like a traffic counter that counts the number of cars passing a certain point in a certain time. If the counter measured 10 cars per second passing a certain point, it would not notice if the cars were moving slowly or quickly.

Electrifying Forces *(cont.)*

Electricity *(cont.)*

It would not notice if the cars were on a four-lane highway or a one-lane road, but only how many passed that certain point in a given time.

How is the power of the circuit measured? It is measured by using a mathematical formula. If we multiply the voltage in a circuit by the number of amps flowing in the circuit, we get the amount of power in a circuit. By increasing the voltage, making the electrons go faster under more pressure, or increasing the number of electrons going past some point in the circuit in a second—or both—the power increases. Power is the amount of work done each second and is measured in a unit called watts. Every electrical item that uses house electrical power has a plate on it somewhere that tells how much power it uses. It may also tell the voltage and the current ratings of the device.

Electric Meters

Electricity is very important in our lives. It can be very useful, and most people cannot imagine what life would be like without all the electrical appliances in our homes today. Refrigerators, televisions, and stereos are examples of appliances powered by electricity. Electric meters are the devices used by the electric companies to keep track of the number of kilowatt hours used in homes.

The meters may be found on the outside of a home or on the inside, perhaps in a basement. Each meter has five dials. The first dial on the right has the numbers zero to nine around the dial in a clockwise order. Dials three and five are arranged in the same order as dial one. The dials that are second and fourth from the right have zero to nine on their face arranged in counterclockwise order. All of the dials are covered by a clear plastic case that enables them to be read easily and be protected from adverse weather conditions. When the dials are read by meter readers from the electric company, they are read from left to right, with each number having a place value. If the meter below was read, the dials would show 24,791 kilowatts.

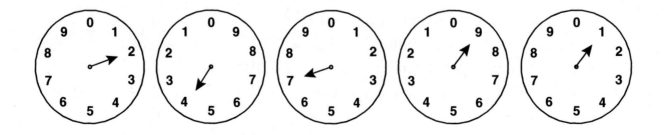

Electrifying Forces *(cont.)*

Electric Meters *(cont.)*

The electric company usually reads the meter each month and computes the difference between the reading for the current month and the prior month. The numbers on the electric meter increase in value as more electricity is used. This means that a meter having a higher number would indicate that it is a more recent reading. The electric company computes a homeowner's bill by finding the difference between kilowatt hours used during current and previous month and multiplying the difference by the rate the company charges. For example, if a customer had a meter with a September reading of 29,481 kilowatt hours and the meter reading for August was 28,240 kilowatt hours, by subtracting the two readings we would find that that customer used 1,241 kilowatt hours between the August and September reading. If the electric company charged five cents per kilowatt hour, to compute the cost of the kilowatt hours used, we would multiply the usage by the rate. In this case, the usage is 1,241 kilowatt hours and the rate is five cents per hour. The total bill would be $62.05.

The electric company sends a bill to the customer each month, along with an explanation of the charges. Some electric companies compare a customer's kilowatt-hour use to the use at the same time the previous year. They may also compare a customer's use to the average use of kilowatt hours by other customers they serve. This gives the customer a gauge to judge if his reading is within a normal range.

Electrifying Forces *(cont.)*

A. Define current, voltage, and power. Explain how they are measured.

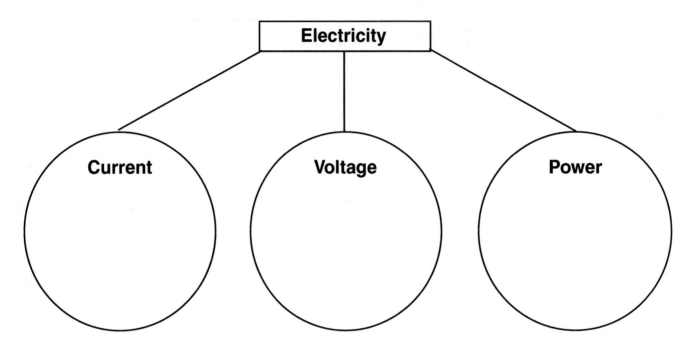

B. What is the difference between high voltage and low voltage?

_____

_____

_____

_____

_____

_____

_____

_____

_____

_____

Electrifying Forces *(cont.)*

C. Read the meters below for November and December. If the electric company charges three cents per kilowatt hour, what will the total bill be for this customer?

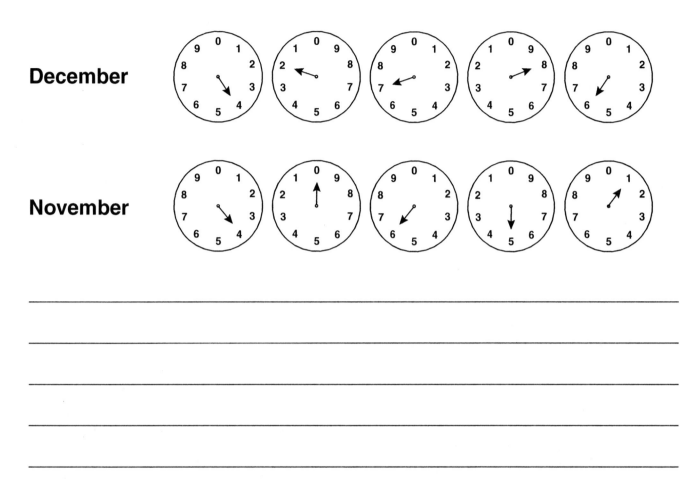

_____

_____

_____

_____

_____

Planning Section

Use the space below to plan your response to the essay question that appears on the following page. You may use a graphic organizer or web to help you plan your essay. Write your final essay on the lines provided below the essay question.

Electrifying Forces *(cont.)*

Essay

The demand for electricity has increased over the last 15 years.

In your essay include:

★ why the demand for electric power has increased

★ two electrically powered appliances that most homes have today

★ three ways that people can conserve electricity

Be sure to check for correct spelling, punctuation, and grammar.

_____

_____

_____

_____

_____

_____

_____

_____

_____

_____

_____

_____

Charting Power Usage

You are going to read two articles about energy. The first one, "Picture This," is about different ways to display information. The second selection, "Seeing The Whole Trend," will show you what the same information looks like when it is presented in different formats.

First you will complete a chart and two short-response questions. Then you will write an essay about the two articles. You may look back at the articles as of often as necessary.

Picture This

People in all fields of study may be involved in collecting information or data. Perhaps, after doing a science experiment or a math problem, you will be asked to present the data you have gathered in a way that will be meaningful to others viewing it. Then, you will be faced with deciding how to do this most effectively. There are many times when every single piece of information is important. Then again, there are other times when the general results of the data are more important than one or two individual pieces of information.

Lists are good ways of organizing information in sequence, perhaps from highest to lowest in value, importance, or from most recent to distant past. The problem with a list is that it may be long and very difficult to interpret. It is very important to be able to see the general results of the data. This can be achieved by grouping the data together and displaying it in a more meaningful format. This format can take the shape of a chart.

Some charts are better for describing a particular data set than others. Often, the best way to organize data when it is first collected is as a table. A table contains all data in raw form. The problem with a table is that some information, such as trends, is not easily seen. Also, if the table is quite large, the amount of data can become overwhelming.

In a situation where it is important to see the impact of the data rather than the data itself, plotting the data graphically is a better choice. There are three types of graphs that are most commonly used: the bar graph, the line graph, and the pie graph.

Charting Power Usage *(cont.)*

Picture This *(cont.)*

The bar graph is a block-form line chart. It shows trends well and makes comparing a few data points near each other easy. For example, it is easy to see that certain points on the graph are lower or higher than others. However, the bar graph tends to get messy if there are too many data points.

The line graph shows trends very well and can include as many data points as necessary. However, it is generally not as appealing to people and seldom includes color. It also may be harder to read individual data points exactly.

The pie graph shows how values relate to one another very well. It is also easy to understand and is appealing to people. However, only a few data groups can be shown on one graph.

Whether you use a list, chart, or graph, each one is suited to help the viewer understand the data more easily. The choice you make is determined by the type and amount of information you will present, as well as the task at hand.

Charting Power Usage *(cont.)*

Seeing the Whole Trend

A picture can help you see things clearly. This page contains information about the power used in Hyteque City. The same data is presented to you four different ways: as a table, a bar graph, a line graph, and a pie graph.

Table Showing Raw Data for Power Usage for Hyteque City

Power Usage for Hyteque City							
Time	Megawatts	Time	Megawatts	Time	Megawatts	Time	Megawatts
12 A.M.	7	1 A.M.	6	2 A.M.	5	3 A.M.	5
4 A.M.	6	5 A.M.	7	6 A.M.	10	7 A.M.	14
8 A.M.	21	9 A.M.	24	10 A.M.	25	11 A.M.	24
12 P.M.	26	1 P.M.	25	2 P.M.	26	3 P.M.	25
4 P.M.	24	5 P.M.	23	6 P.M.	18	7 P.M.	15
8 P.M.	14	9 P.M.	12	10 P.M.	10	11 P.M.	9

Bar Graph Showing Power Usage for Hyteque City

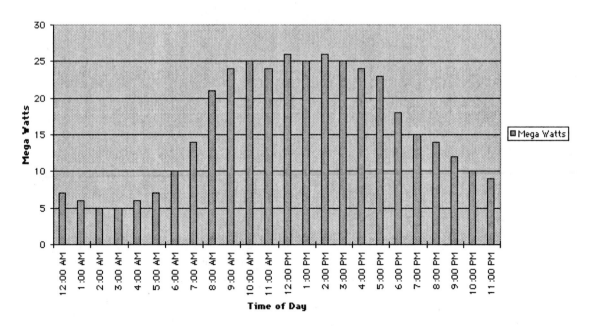

Power Usage for Hyteque City

Charting Power Usage *(cont.)*

Line Graph Showing Power usage for Hyteque City

Power Usage for Hyteque City

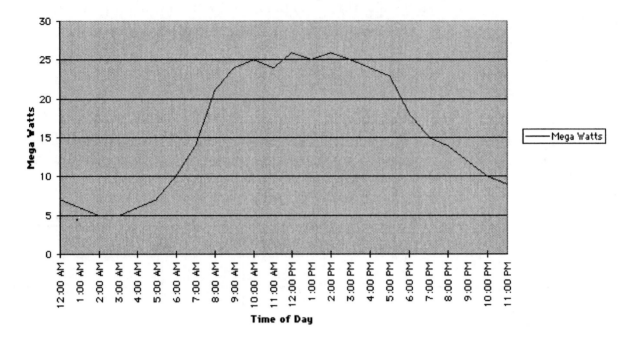

Pie Graph Showing Power Usage for Hyteque City

Day vs. Night Power Usage

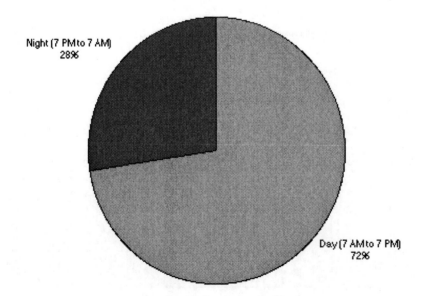

Night (7 PM to 7 AM)
28%

Day (7 AM to 7 PM)
72%

Charting Power Usage *(cont.)*

A. Compare bar graphs and line graphs.

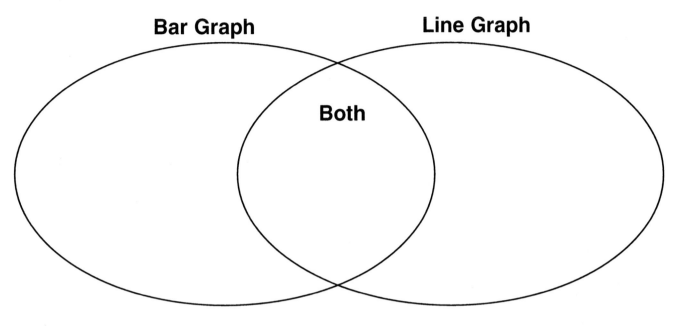

Bar Graph   **Line Graph**

Both

B. Between what hours is the demand greatest for power in Hyteque City? Where was this information most easily located?

_____

_____

_____

_____

_____

_____

_____

_____

_____

_____

_____

Charting Power Usage *(cont.)*

C. When would you need to use a table, bar graph, line graph, or pie graph in your life? Give specific examples.

_____

_____

_____

_____

_____

_____

_____

_____

_____

Planning Selection

Use the space below to plan your response to the essay question that appears on the following page. You may use a graphic organizer or web to help you plan your essay. Write your final essay on the lines provided below the essay question.

Charting Power Usage *(cont.)*

Essay

Just like Hyteque City, many cities have increased demand for power usage during certain times of the day or during certain times of the year.

★ Name one time of the year that there is a greater demand for power and explain why this occurs.

★ Name two problems that are caused by the greater demand.

★ Name two ways that people can conserve energy and lessen this demand.

Be sure to check your paper for correct spelling, grammar and punctuation.

_____

_____

_____

_____

_____

_____

_____

_____

_____

_____

_____

_____

_____

Essay Paper

_____

_____

_____

_____

_____

_____

_____

_____

_____

_____

_____

_____

_____

_____

_____

_____

_____

_____

_____

Answer Key

pages 15–17 (National Holidays)

A. Accept the following answers in any order: Julia Ward Howe, Mary Towers Sasseen, Frank E. Hering, Anna Jarvis, Woodrow Wilson.

B. In May of 1914, President Woodrow Wilson signed a resolution recommending that the government recognize and observe Mother's Day as a national holiday. The government declared it a national holiday in 1915—to be observed on the second Sunday in May—as selected by Anna Jarvis who urged the celebration from 1908 until its adoption.

C. Sonora Dodd, after hearing about a Mother's Day holiday, wanted to honor her own father, William Smart, who had raised six children alone after his wife died. She began a petition in Spokane, Washington to adopt an annual Father's Day celebration. She received support from several organizations, and the first Father's Day was officially celebrated on June 19, 1910.

Essay: Answers will vary. Accept all reasonable essays that include information that highlights each topic.

pages 21–23 (Female Civil Rights Leaders)

A. Answers could include terms, such as brave, courageous, kind, caring, determined, self-reliant, sympathetic, good, thoughtful, daring, adventuresome, heroic, fearless, unafraid, gallant, etc.

B. After Rosa Parks took a seat in the rear of the bus, she was asked to leave her seat for a white man because all the seats were filled. Rosa Parks refused to move. The bus driver stopped the bus and called the police. The police arrested Rosa Parks, and NAACP leader, Edgar Nixon, posted bail for her. A one day boycott of all city buses was declared. The boycott was extended and lasted 381 days, until the Supreme Court declared bus segregation unconstitutional.

C. Accept any reasonable answer that includes that Harriet Tubman, born a slave in Maryland, was able to get North to Philadelphia, Pennsylvania, by means of the Underground Railroad, a network of roads, tunnels, and homes that were used to take slaves to freedom. The Underground Railroad was run by people that believed slavery was wrong. After she was free, Harriet Tubman worked to help others reach freedom.

Essay: Answers will vary. Accept any reasonable response.

pages 28–30 (Power of Women)

A. Answers could include the following ideas:
Pat Nixon—kind, supported volunteerism
Betty Ford—honest, truthful about personal problems such as breast cancer and alcohol addiction.
Rosalynn Carter—smart, participated in cabinet meetings, trustworthy, represented U.S. in Central America

B. Pat Nixon supported volunteerism, the idea that Americans should get involved in their communities.

Betty Ford supported the Equal Rights Amendment, research and education about breast cancer, and drug and alcohol awareness.

Rosalynn Carter supported mental health reform, social-security reform, and the Equal Rights Amendment.

Answer Key *(cont.)*

C. The Equal Rights Amendment was to be the 27th Amendment to the Constitution. It called for the complete legal equality between the sexes. That meant women were to be treated the same way in the work place as men. Educational institutions, which received funds from the federal government, would lose aid if they discriminated on the basis of sex. Many states have passed laws that require this type of legal treatment.

Essay: Answers will vary. Accept all reasonable responses.

pages 34—36 (Marine Disasters)

A.

Main Ideas	*Titanic*	*Lusitania*
Departure Point/Date	Southampton, England/April 1912	New York/May 1, 1915
Destination	New York City	Liverpool, England
Number of Passengers/Crew	2,200	1,959
Death Toll	1,517	1,200
Cause of Destruction	iceberg	torpedo

B. The people on board the *Titanic* weren't rescued before the ship sank because the ship, the *California*, which was only 20 minutes away, didn't respond to the distress signal: the radio operator was not on duty. The *Carpathia*, another ship, was four hours away, too far to be of help to most people. By the time it arrived, it was two hours after the *Titanic* split in half.

C. The United States was not involved in WWI when the Lusitania set sail. Germans torpedoed the ship near the coast of Ireland. The boat sank in 18 minutes. The Germans had orders to sink all ships headed for Great Britain. President Wilson protested the attack. The German government apologized for the error, but Americans were angry and America entered the Great War.

Essay: Answers will vary. Accept any reasonable essays that target each bulleted topic.

pages 41–43 (Freedom Rings)

A. Types of freedoms include: physical, political, social, intellectual, and personal. Symbols include: bridges, victory gardens, flags, doves, lights, and birds.

B. During WWII, people in America planted gardens of vegetables in any space they could find in order to produce more food. It was needed to help the war effort. The gardens became symbols of an individual's support of the causes of his or her government. It was a very patriotic effort on the part of the Americans across the country.

C. All bridges symbolize possibilities of travel that once didn't exist and also symbolize man's unending capabilities of creativity. The Golden Gate Bridge was built in 1937 at the entrance to the San Francisco Bay in California. It is a monumental symbol of freedom of travel and ability because of how big it is and how much it cost to build. It is 4200 feet long and 90 feet wide. It cost $35.5 billion to build in 1937. In addition, it stands as an entry on the West Coast of the United States, the greatest country of freedom in the world.

Essay: Answers will vary. Accept any reasonable response. Responses will include ideas about color, stripes, stars, and objects that appear on the flags.

Answer Key *(cont.)*

pages 46–48 (The Great World Wars)

A. *Cause and Date*—assassination of Archduke Ferdinand and his wife, Sophie; June 1914

Allied Powers—Russia, Great Britain, France, U.S.

Results of the Peace Treaty of Versailles—established independent countries of Poland, Czechoslovakia, and Yugoslavia; set up the League of Nations and excluded Germany from its membership

Central Powers—Germany, Austria-Hungary, Italy

B. The Peace Treaty of Versailles had both positive and negative results. The positive results included three main ideas: it created three newly independent countries, countries could settle and discuss issues at the League of Nations, and it marked the end of the war. There were also three negative aspects. Germany was excluded from the League of Nations. Germany was left on her own to rebuild. Lastly, Germany became hostile because of the other issues.

C. There were three main results of the bombing of Pearl Harbor: First, it brought the United States into World War II. Second, men between the ages of 21–35 had to register for possible draft into the army. Finally, there was a major opening of the workforce for women in factory jobs related to the war effort.

Essay: Answers will vary. Accept all reasonable answers.

pages 53–55 (Decades of Change)

A. Accept reasonable answers.

B. According to the author, the Roaring '20s was a time of great opportunity. The economy expanded because World War I ended. Much more money was available for other aspects of the economy besides the military. Many new jobs developed and were being promoted. Finally, the entertainment industry opened and saw a remarkable growth spurt.

C. The Great Depression was the period of time from 1929–1939. It received its name due to the conditions that existed in this country. There was a depressed economy and much hardship for all people in the United States. The mood of the people was also depressed. People lost a lot of money, and many banks failed and closed.

Essay: Answers will vary. Accept all reasonable answers that are expressed in the categories of lifestyle, jobs, economy, and location.

Answer Key (cont.)

pages 60–62 (Documenting Through Photography)

A. 1920—unemployment, hunger, despair

1930s—Farm Security Administration

1934—books, magazine articles, exhibits

1945—United Nations Conference

B. Accept all reasonable answers. Some acceptable responses might include the following emotions: pity, compassion, fear, unhappiness, revulsion, and pride. Examples to support the emotions chosen would include pictures of unemployed people, the Dust Bowl, Japanese internment camps, and country women.

C. The farmers of the Dust Bowl faced many problems due to nature and their own negligence. Windstorms and long periods of drought were problems of nature of which they had no control. The farmers, however, were also negligent. They misused the land by depleting the soil, moving to new land, and plowing up natural grasses to plant wheat. In addition, the farmers ignored conservationists' tactics to prevent erosion. They did not heed the advice about contour plowing or planting trees to prevent wind erosion.

Essay: Answers will vary. Accept all reasonable responses.

pages 65–67 (Ancient Greek Heroes)

A. Accept all reasonable answers.

B. Answers will vary. Accept any response that is supported with details and an explanation.

C. The Greeks defeated the Trojans by building a very large wooden horse. Fifty Greek soldiers hid inside the horse. The rest of the Greek army brought the horse near the walls of Troy and then snuck away. The Trojans wanted to explore this huge object, so they brought it within the walls of the city of Troy. At night, the Greek soldiers emerged, surprising and defeating the Trojans.

Essay: Answers will vary. Accept all reasonable responses that relate to the myths Hercules and Helen of Troy.

pages 71—73 (Courageous Women)

A. First female doctor. Received medical degree from Geneva Medical School in 1849. Established New York Infirmary for Women and Children in 1857. Founded London School of Medicine in England in 1869. Blackwell Medal of Recognition named in honor of Dr. Elizabeth Blackwell.

Answer Key *(cont.)*

B. Karana was imagining that she fashioned or created weapons. The laws of her tribe forbid women from making weapons of any kind. She was worried that three natural disasters might occur as a result of her transgressions. Major winds from the four corners of the world might converge, an earthquake might cover her with rocks, or a tidal wave might flood the island. Karana was concerned about the problems that might arise from the natural disasters, as well as the consequences of breaking the laws of her people.

C. Sandra Day O'Connor had to overcome many obstacles in reaching her goals. Discrimination in the male-dominated profession of law was extensive when she wanted to become an attorney. Ms. O'Connor had difficulty getting into law school. After graduating with honors, she had a hard time finding a job as a lawyer. Ms. O'Connor faced formidable opponents when running for the Arizona State Senate. Finally, when she was nominated as a justice to the Supreme Court, she had to surmount the investigative process and win approval by Congress. Despite the obstacles in her path, Ms. Sandra Day O'Connor reached her goals at each challenge.

Essay: Answers will vary. Accept all reasonable responses.

pages 78–80 (Art Appreciation)

A.

1. sketched a scene
2. individual drawings of each element in scene
3. full-sized charcoal drawings
4. color sketches
5. painting

B. Norman Rockwell pursued the following path to attain his success and recognition as an American painter:

1. drew pictures to entertain classmates during school years
2. studied at the National Academy of Design
3. drew designs for greeting cards
4. studied at the Art Students League
5. began illustrating books and magazines
6. at 18, became art director of *Boys' Life* Magazine (Boy Scouts magazine)
7. created the 318 covers for *Saturday Evening Post* over a 47-year period and painted for the Navy during WWI
8. worked for Look Magazine
9. paintings and collection on display at the Norman Rockwell Museum in Stockbridge, Massachusetts and worldwide

C. Henri Matisse had planned on becoming an attorney. While in training to become a lawyer, he required surgery. During his recuperation period, his mother brought him paints and a how-to book. After he recovered, he went to Paris to study painting with the support and encouragement of his mother but not his father.

Essay: Answers will vary. Accept all reasonable responses.

Answer Key *(cont.)*

pages 83–85 (Open Arms)

A. **Seven Continents**

1. North America
2. South America
3. Europe
4. Asia
5. Africa
6. Australia
7. Antarctica

Seven Liberties

1. civil liberty
2. moral liberty
3. national liberty
4. natural liberty
5. personal liberty
6. political liberty
7. religious liberty

B. Three reasons that immigrants came to America were to find better jobs; to see a better way of life; and to escape persecution, war, starvation and/or disease.

In seeking better jobs they were looking for personal liberty. When looking for a better way of life they were looking for moral, natural, and person liberty. Depending on what type of persecution they were seeking to escape they may have been seeking all of the liberties.

C. The types of immigrants that the Statue of Liberty welcomed were the tired, the poor, and the homeless who had journeyed far to get to the land of liberty.

pages 89–91 (Being An Individual)

A. 1900—tested glider that could hold one person
1901—tested larger glider
1902—tested glider, that flew over 600 feet
1903—flew power airplane at Kitty Hawk
1905—tested a plane that flew 24.2 miles in 38 minutes
1908—signed contract with U.S. Department of War to build first military airplane

B. The Wright Brothers built and sold homemade mechanical toys, built a printing press and began a printing business, published a newspaper, rented and sold bicycles, built bicycles, and built gliders and airplanes.

C. The conditions that injured British soldiers faced during the Crimean War were extremely poor. The hospital was surrounded by mud with everything dirty and falling about. There were rats. There were not enough beds, so many soldiers lay on the floor. There were few hospital supplies and soldiers often went without food and medicine. Nurses were not welcomed and were not allowed to help the soldiers. There was often not enough clothing, blankets, or equipment.

To make these conditions better, Florence Nightingale went against Army regulations and purchased supplies. She had the hospital scrubbed and cleaned. She had patients' clothing washed. She attended to administrative duties as well as caring for the sick and dying.

Essay: Answers will vary. Accept all reasonable responses.

Answer Key *(cont.)*

pages 96–98 (Teeing Off)

A. Nancy Lopez—*Problems and Obstacles:* mother ill with lung disorder, no babysitter, needed golf clubs, local country club wouldn't sponsor her, style criticized

Training: father taught her and gave her golf lessons

Accomplishments: won New Mexico Pee Wee tournament; at 11 years of age, played in New Mexico Amateur Tournament; in 1977 won Women's Pro Rookie of the Year Award; by 1995 held in 47 professional tournament championships; member of the LPGA (Ladies Professional Golf Association); inducted into the Hall of Fame

Lee Trevino—*Problems and Obstacles:* poor, picked cotton and onions with grandfather, had to hunt for food, earned money by picking up golf balls, hit by lightning in 1975, required back surgery and rehabilitation

Training: spent hours on a closed golf course practicing with greens keeper's son, played with caddies, was a Marine

Accomplishments: designed and landscaped a nine-hole golf course for Hardy Greenwood, in 1968 won professional tour at U.S. Open, in 1970 led PGA (Professional Golf Association) in earnings, in 1970 won 2nd U.S. Open and Canadian and British Opens, in 1971 selected PGA Player and Sportsman of the Year, in 1979, inducted to the Hall of Fame in 1981, in 1990 won seven out of 26 PGA Senior Tour events.

B. Nancy Lopez's family supported her in her desire to learn to play golf and become a success at the sport. Her mother, though ill, would bring her to all her lessons and practices. She also gave Nancy her golf clubs. Her father was her teacher and coach, providing her with golf lessons.

C. Lee Trevino could be considered a self-made man because he came from a very poor family and he became a very successful and rich athlete. Not only did he earn much money, but he also won many of the professional golf tournaments over the years. He was also recognized with many awards for his ability. (Supporting details will vary.)

Essay: Answers will vary. Accept all reasonable responses.

pages 102–104 (On Ice)

A. Torvill—began skating at age 9, first partner was Michael Hutchinson

Dean—began skating at age 10, first partner Sandra Elson, junior dance champion in 1974

Both—born in Nottingham, England; middle class backgrounds; Janet Sawbridge was coach and trainer; coached by Betty Callaway; in 1978 British ice skating champions; in 1981 won three ice skating competitions; in 1984 skated to *Bolero* in the Olympics and received a perfect score; in 1984 joined the Ice Capades; in 1994 won a Bronze medal at the Olympics

B. Skaters originally performed rigid routines, tracing patterns on ice. Jackson Haines created a single-unit skate with a blade screwed to the sole. He also added ballet, music, and costumes to the sport. He introduced his skating style in Europe in 1864, and the world became as thrilled with the sport as Americans were.

C. Answers will vary, but could include any of the following characteristics: determined, hard working, cooperative, talented, and athletic. Specific examples to support choices will vary.

Essay: Answers will vary. Accept all reasonable responses.

Answer Key *(cont.)*

pages 109–111 (Exploring Above and Below)

A. bathysphere   aqualung and SCUBA gear
bathyscaphe   diving suits
oxygen tanks and mouthpiece with hose

B. The original modern diving equipment consisted of cylinders of oxygen on the divers' backs attached to the mouthpiece with a hose. The tank held enough oxygen for two hours only. The breathing equipment was difficult to use. In addition, pure oxygen below a certain depth turned into a poisonous gas called carbon monoxide. The newer Aqualung helped alleviate the problems.

C. John Glenn's problem was the heat shield. It was located on the bottom of the space capsule and was supposed to protect the astronaut from extreme heat that could be experienced upon reentry into the atmosphere. When Glenn was ready to reenter the Earth's atmosphere in *Friendship 7,* the heat shield loosened. If it had separated, he would have been burned to death. Fortunately, it did not separate and he landed safely in the ocean.

Essay: Answers will vary. Accept all reasonable responses.

pages 115–117 (Technological Advancements)

Invention	Abbreviation	Contribution
video cassette recorder	VCR	tape program for later viewing, expanded entertainment industry, enhances education
compact disc	CD	enhanced sound of recorded music
personal computer	PC	entertainment, shopping, research, education, general productivity and communication worldwide.

B. In the past, viewing of movies was at the discretion of TV producers or viewing in movie theatres. With VCRs, people could buy or rent movies of choice to be viewed at their leisure. Taping of TV movies or shows for later viewing has become very popular, especially with people's busy schedules. Also, many people can now watch one show and tape another to see later. In addition, new businesses developed. Stores that deal with renting and purchasing movies opened. Production companies grew.

C. Television was and still is called the "idiot box" or "boob tube," because some claim that television shows have little value. Television viewing hinders homework completion and many times is done in lieu of reading. There is much violence and sex depicted in some programs, which is inappropriate for children. Television viewing also places undue strain on eyesight.

Essay: Answers will vary. Accept all reasonable responses.

pages 122–124 (Earth's Natural Biomes)

A. Freshwater—plants, snails, crayfish, bass, rooted plants, fungi, insects, frogs, fish, birds, snakes
Saltwater—starfish, kelp, crabs, protozoa, small fish, predator fish, sharks, rays, whales, dolphins
Both—algae, plankton, worms, bacteria

Answer Key *(cont.)*

B. There are two different types of freshwater biomes: running water sources and still-water or standing water sources. Running water includes rivers and streams. It contains more dissolved oxygen than in still water but lacks nutrients for plankton survival. Plants need to anchor to rocks or pebbles. Fish have streamlined bodies. Still-water sources include lakes and ponds, where rooted plants are common, plankton and algae are abundant, and much animal life exists, like insects, frogs, fish, birds, and snakes.

C. The ground of the tundra is called permafrost because it is permanently frozen. Only the top layer thaws during the summer months. The plant life that lives in the tundra has short roots and gets enough nutrition from the small amount of soil that has thawed. Trees have very extensive root systems that cannot grow in the permafrost.

Essay: Answers will vary. Accept all reasonable responses.

pages 128–130 (Plants)

A. *Simple Plants: Location*—everywhere in nature (freshwater, saltwater, soil, on animals). *Structure*—non-vascular, grow in clumps or mats. Characteristics—make their own food or live off a host, grow close to the ground and in clumps or mats grow quickly, no embryos. *Examples*—algae, fungi like yeast, mushrooms, and bacteria.

Complex Plants: *Location*—on land. *Structure*—vascular, have bundles of xylem and phloem. *Characteristics*—make their own food through photosynthesis, reproduce through embryos, grow tall and wide. *Examples*—deciduous trees, conifers, ferns, and flowering plants.

B. One of the major differences between simple and complex plants is the structure. Simple plants have neither xylem nor phloem, like the complex plants do. The xylem and phloem are tube-like structures. The xylem carries water and minerals up through the stem to the leaves, while the phloem carries the dissolved food down from the leaves, where it was made, to other parts of the plant. Simple plants grow close to the ground due to their structure. Complex plants grow tall and wide due to their structure.

C. Elements necessary for the successful growth of a plant include water, minerals, and sunlight. A plant gets the water and minerals it needs from the soil. Its root system absorbs the water and minerals and they travel upwards to fortify the rest of the plant. The roots anchor the plant and continue to grow downwards because of the pull of gravity. The stem and leaves of the plant grow upwards toward the sunlight, which enables the plant to produce its own food through the process of photosynthesis. Green plants are able to combine the carbon dioxide from the air, the water and minerals from the soil, and use their own chlorophyll to produce their own food.

Essay: Answers will vary. Accept all reasonable responses.

pages 134–136 (Splitting Genes)

A. *Obstacles:* tomboy, parents didn't want her to go to college; no assistants to help her in her work

Areas of Study: botany and genetics.

Awards: honorary doctorate from Harvard University, McArthur Laureate Award

Answer Key *(cont.)*

B. Gregor Mendel's work helped people understand the science of inherited characteristics because he expounded the theory that some genes were dominant and others were recessive. The dominant, or stronger, genes mask the appearance of the recessive, or weaker, genes. He also said that since the genes were found in pairs, one was contributed from each parent. The offspring had the result of the combination of parent genes. His work with pea plants was adapted to human genetics.

C. A dominant gene is the stronger gene. A recessive gene is a weaker gene. The dominant gene covers or masks the characteristic of the recessive, or weaker, gene.

Essay: Answers will vary. Accept all reasonable responses.

pages 140–142 (Electrifying Forces)

A. *Current:* movement of electrons, more movement means greater current, measured in amps, regulated by resistors that change the flow

Voltage: electrons push forward, pushing power or force, high voltage equals greater force and greater number of electrons, low voltage equals few electrons or a weak force, measured in volts

Power: voltage times amps equals power, amount of work done each second is a watt, power increases with electrons going faster under pressure or increased number of electrons.

B. Low voltage means there are only a few electrons pushing, yielding a weak force. High voltage means electrons are pushing harder.

C. December—42786

November—40651

$$\begin{array}{r} 2135 \\ \times\ .03 \\ \hline \$64.05 \end{array}$$

$64.05 equals total cost for the month from November through December.

Essay: Answers will vary. Accept all reasonable responses.

pages 147–149 (Charting Power Usage)

A. **Bar Graph:** block-form line graph, points near each other are easily compared, messy if there are too many data points

Line Graph: includes as many data points as necessary, not appealing to many people, generally no use of color, hard to read exact data points

Both graphs: show trends well, visual representation, more appealing than charts, easier to read than text

B. The greatest demand for power in Hyteque City is between the hours of 8:00 A.M. and 6:00 P.M. The answer to the question about where the information was most easily located will vary from student to student.

C. Answers will vary. Accept all reasonable responses.

Essay: Answers will vary. Accept all reasonable responses.